TSIA2™ BOOT CAMP
Better Scores in ONE Day

Oliver Pope

Inquiries concerning this publication should be mailed to:

MasteryPrep

7117 Florida Blvd.

Baton Rouge, LA 70806

MasteryPrep is a trade name and/or trademark of Ring Publications LLC.

10 9 8 7 6 5 4 3 2 1

ISBN-13: 978-1-948846-79-0

A Note From MasteryPrep

Since 2013, MasteryPrep has helped over 300,000 students improve their scores on the most popular standardized tests, including ACT, SAT, WorkKeys, STAAR, and the TSIA2. We specialize in helping students who aren't "good test takers" get the scores they need for the school, scholarship, or job they're interested in.

This Boot Camp was written to help you. If you had a private tutor, you might ask, "I'm taking my TSIA2 in two days. What do I need to know?" The information in this workshop is exactly what you would be given. This program is designed to give you the ultimate one-day cram. With this Boot Camp, you can learn the skills that you need to boost your scores on the TSIA2.

Most students we've worked with seem to do best under pressure. You can call it simply "waiting until the last minute," but we think there is a human instinct that kicks in, a survival mechanism of sorts, that clears your head and helps you do what needs to get done.

This workshop is for the "final hours." It's here because, sometimes, the best prep comes just before the test begins. This Boot Camp will guide you through the essentials on content, test-taking strategies, and the most common question types on the TSIA2.

At MasteryPrep, we've done research based on what students most need to do well on the TSIA2 and have distilled that information down into this workshop. It's designed to give you everything you need—and nothing that you don't—quickly enough that you can cover it all in a single day.

Good luck!

TABLE OF CONTENTS

ORIENTATION

WHY PREPARE FOR THE TSIA2?

The most important prep you need for the TSIA2 has nothing to do with the test itself: You will increase your score tremendously if you find your **motivation**.

This will be different for each person, but here are a few things to keep in mind:

- **The TSIA2 will save you money:** If you achieve a high score on the TSIA2, you may be able to skip introductory courses or take them as part of Dual Credit in high school, which will save you money.
- **The TSIA2 will save you time:** Every course you test out of is one less course you have to take in order to graduate college.
- **The TSIA2 will help you earn your degree:** Studies show that students who place out of introductory courses can be five times as likely to finish their degrees.

It's up to you to get motivated. If you can find your personal *why*, we can work together on the *how*.

NOTES:

_____

_____

_____

_____

_____

_____

_____

_____

_____

_____

ORIENTATION

The TSIA2 is actually two different tests, each with its own set of questions and separate scores. The TSIA2 is **not** a timed test, and you can start or stop the test whenever you like—but expect to spend up to 3–4 hours on the entire exam.

SUBJECT	QUESTIONS	SCORE RANGE
English Language Arts and Reading		
Multiple Choice	30	910 to 990
Essay	1	1 to 8
Mathematics		
Multiple Choice	20	910 to 990

The **English Language Arts and Reading (ELAR)** test measures your reading comprehension ability as well as your ability to edit sentences and write an essay in response to a prompt.

The **Mathematics** test measures your ability to solve multiple-choice math questions from Algebra, Geometry, and Statistics.

NOTES:

_____

_____

_____

_____

_____

_____

_____

_____

HOW THE TSIA2 IS SCORED

The TSIA2 is a computer-adaptive test, which means a few things for you:

- As you do better on the test, the questions get **harder**, and your score goes **up**.
- As you do worse on the test, the questions get **easier**, but your score goes **down**.
- Each question is presented one at a time, and you **can't** return to previous questions.

There are some methods you can use to take advantage of this fact:

- **Be Prepared:** The first question will be of medium difficulty, and the test will adapt from there, so be ready.
- **Focus Early:** The score on an adaptive test is usually affected by the **first** questions a lot more than the **final** questions.
- **Don't Stress:** The test will get harder as you do better, so don't give up when you see more difficult questions—that means you're actually on the right track!

NOTES:

_____

_____

_____

_____

_____

_____

_____

_____

_____

MAKING THE CUT

The TSIA2 is scored on a scale between 910 and 990. In order to pass the test, you will need to hit a different cut score for each part of the overall exam.

SUBJECT	PASSING SCORE
English Language Arts and Reading	
Multiple Choice	945+
Essay*	5+
Mathematics	
Multiple Choice	950+

If you fail to make the cut score on any of the tests, you will be given a **Diagnostic Test**. If you score high enough on the Diagnostic Test, you can still pass the benchmark. Since the Diagnostic Test is harder to prepare for, we will only focus on helping you pass the Multiple-Choice section.

The essay will only be given if you score at least a 945 on the multiple-choice section of the ELAR or at least a 4 on the Diagnostic Test.

NOTES:

_____

_____

_____

_____

_____

_____

_____

_____

PACE YOURSELF

Because the TSIA2 is an **untimed** test, there is no need to rush anything on the exam. You can even pause a section (except for the essay) and return to it at any point.

- **Take Your Time:** Read everything carefully. Solve every math problem by showing your work. Try out answer choices if you are stuck. Do what it takes to give your best effort on **every** question.
- **Use Mental Breaks**: After every few questions, close your eyes and take a quick mental break. Even a few seconds can recharge your focus.
- **Leave the Room:** Remember that you can stop and start at any time during a section, so feel free to pause halfway and take a walk around to refuel your brain before you finish the section.
- **Stay Alert:** Finally, don't let the unlimited time trick you into being a passive test-taker—you still need to be actively involved in the process, even if you have no time restrictions.

NOTES:

_____

_____

_____

_____

_____

_____

_____

_____

_____

_____

GET READY FOR TEST DAY

Before you can take your test, you must take care of a couple things:

- **First**, you must take the **pre-assessment**. This sounds intimidating, but it's just a survey to make sure you understand the rules of the TSIA2 and how it affects your application to college. You don't need to study for it.

- **Second**, you must pick the date you will take your test. Some centers will require you to **schedule** your test. Others will allow you to take it without an appointment, but you **must** give them at least four hours before they close—otherwise they might not let you take it that day.

At the end of the Boot Camp, we will go over some more tips for getting mentally ready the day before the test, but you should start with these two crucial steps.

NOTES:

_____

_____

_____

_____

_____

_____

_____

_____

_____

BIG PICTURE TEST-TAKING HABITS

The TSIA2 covers two distinct tests—the ELAR and Mathematics tests—but there are some general test-taking habits you should keep in mind across the whole exam.

- **Process of Elimination:** Find the correct answer by focusing on eliminating the wrong ones. There are **three times** as many wrong answers as correct ones, so they're easier to find.

- **Always Check Twice:** Double-check your work, whether it is a math solution, a grammar rule, or eliminated answers on a Reading passage. Remember—you have unlimited time!

- **One at a Time:** You can only work on the question in front of you, so don't worry about how you did on past questions or what may come up in future questions. Focus on what's in front of you and keep moving.

NOTES:

_____

_____

_____

_____

_____

_____

_____

_____

_____

_____

_____

SECTION TWO

ENGLISH LANGUAGE ARTS AND READING

An Introduction to the TSIA2 ELAR Test

The TSIA2 ELAR (English Language Arts and Reading) test is made up of 30 multiple-choice questions and an essay. We are going to discuss the multiple-choice section first.

The two areas of focus for the multiple-choice section of the ELAR test are:

Reading Focus

- **Literary Text Analysis:** This category includes questions related to broad concepts such as purpose and point of view as well as specific concepts such as drawing inferences, all in the context of a literary text.

- **Informational Text Analysis and Synthesis:** This category includes questions on broad concepts such as main idea and passage relationships as well as specific concepts such as identifying details in a passage, all in the context of an informational text.

Writing Focus

- **Essay Revision and Editing:** This category includes organization, word choice, and other composition issues as they relate to an essay.

- **Sentence Revision, Editing, and Completion:** This category includes using proper punctuation, grammar, and usage issues in the context of a single sentence.

NOTES:

_____

_____

_____

_____

_____

_____

_____

How to Take the ELAR Test

Before you learn specific strategies for the multiple-choice section of the ELAR test, you need to start with an overall game plan.

The ELAR Game Plan

1. **Identify the Focus and Type**

   There are two focuses: Reading and Writing. Each has its own types of questions.

   - **Reading:** Short Passage, Long Passage, and Dual Passage
   - **Writing:** Sentence Correction and Passage Correction

   We will review specific strategies for each of these types in the next section of the chapter.

2. **Decode the Question**

   For each question, determine:

   - **What** is the question topic? For Writing-focused questions, what rule is on trial? For Reading-focused questions, what is the question asking about, and what does it want to know?
   - **Where** will you need to find the answer? For Writing-focused questions, what do you need from the sentence or essay to make a choice? For Reading-focused questions, which part of the passage will help you answer the question?

3. **Use the Right Strategy**

   Depending on the focus and type of question, you should use the strategy that best fits. We will review many core strategies, so you will have plenty of ways to tackle the questions on the TSIA2 ELAR test.

4. **Use the Process of Elimination**

   Take **two passes** on each set of answer choices:

   - **First Pass:** Eliminate any choices that are obviously wrong.
   - **Second Pass:** Compare the remaining choices and pick the best option.

NOTES:

_____

_____

_____

_____

THREE READING PASSAGE TYPES

The ELAR test makes use of **three** formats for its reading passages, which will alter exactly how the basic strategy is applied.

- **Short Passages:** These passages consist of a single paragraph and a single question.
- **Long Passages:** These passages contain multiple paragraphs and have exactly 3 questions.
- **Dual Passages:** These passages are a combination of two short passages that are related to each other in some way. They have one or two questions.

NOTES:

_____

_____

_____

_____

_____

_____

_____

_____

_____

_____

_____

_____

Two Writing Question Types

While there are a few different writing topics on the TSIA2 ELAR test, there are **exactly two** formats for the questions. Learning them is a key part of your basic approach.

Sentence Correction: These questions will ask you to correct an underlined portion of a sentence.

Passage Correction: These questions provide a passage and a series of questions asking you to restructure sentences in the essay or the entire essay itself.

NOTES:

_____

_____

_____

_____

_____

_____

_____

_____

_____

_____

_____

_____

_____

SECTION TWO, ELAR: SHORT PASSAGE

SHORT PASSAGE, PRACTICE SET ONE

Passage
In 2012, volunteers for "Let's Do It! World," a worldwide movement to combat the global solid waste problem, planned a six-month series of cleanups around the globe. These "cleanup days" occurred in 96 different countries, including Estonia, Lebanon, Nepal, and the Philippines. Slovenia's cleanup day was the largest that year, with over 289,000 participants. The tradition is gaining momentum, and on February 9, 2014, country cleanup leaders from around the world agreed to the goal of involving 380 million people by 2018.

Question 1 of 6
The passage suggests that the main goal of the cleanup days was to encourage people to

	Answers
A	spend more time in nature
B	volunteer for meaningful causes
C	commit to making a cleaner planet
D	travel to neighboring countries

Passage
When we think of blushing, embarrassment, redness, and a rise in temperature come to mind—all noticeable in the face. Most people are surprised to discover the phenomenon of blushing also occurs in the stomach. Because adrenaline causes tiny blood vessels called capillaries to widen and increase blood flow, the tissue around these vessels in the stomach appears as red as a blushing cheek. Though this may seem unnatural to some, the stomach is just another example of how the brain uses chemical processes to prepare the body for fight or flight in often unnoticed ways.

Question 2 of 6
The main idea of the passage is that

	Answers
A	blushing in the face is identical to blushing in the stomach
B	adrenaline causes blood vessels to widen for increased blood flow
C	the stomach is the most prepared part of the body for fight or flight
D	stomach blushing goes unnoticed but is a natural process

Passage
I can still smell the rich aroma of our olive oil. There were so many flavors in it: spicy pepper, the green earthiness of tomato leaves, and a light, banana-like sweetness behind it all. My *nonna* would use it in her marinara and drizzle it on top of gnocchi with parmesan, and it tasted like heaven. It satisfied the palate in a way nothing else could.

Which of the following conclusions about the narrator's response to the aroma can most logically be drawn from the passage?

Answers	
A	She is disappointed over a painful loss.
B	She is delighted by the warmth of a pleasant memory.
C	She is saddened that she is not still living on the family farm.
D	She is filled with satisfaction from completing a difficult task.

The Short Passage Basic Strategy

The topic of a **Short Passage** will vary from passage to passage, but one thing you can count on is that you will have **exactly one question**. We are going to use this to our advantage.

The Basic Strategy

1. **Read the Question First**
    The question won't always give you a great starting point—in fact, it will often just ask for the main idea—but it is always worth reading the question to focus your reading.

2. **Read the Passage**
    If the question has a **specific** topic, read to see what the passage says about the topic.

    If the question asks about the **entire** passage, read all of the passage to get the main idea.

3. **Find Your Evidence**
    Since the passage is short, you can use specific words from the passage to support your answer.

4. **Use the Process of Elimination**
    Eliminate answers as you normally would and keep an eye out for common traps:

    -   **Extreme**: These choices take something mentioned in the passage and exaggerate it.
    -   **True but Irrelevant**: These choices will reference something that is covered in the passage, but is irrelevant to the question.
    -   **Opposite**: These choices will twist words in the passage into something that says the opposite.
    -   **Recycled Language**: These choices will use words from the passage to say something different from the passage.
    -   **Half Right:** These choices will get half of the answer right, but they include something that is specifically wrong as well.

NOTES:

_____

_____

_____

_____

Let's try it out with the first question from the exercise.

Passage
In 2012, volunteers for "Let's Do It! World," a worldwide movement to combat the global solid waste problem, planned a six-month series of cleanups around the globe. These "cleanup days" occurred in 96 different countries, including Estonia, Lebanon, Nepal, and the Philippines. Slovenia's cleanup day was the largest that year, with over 289,000 participants. The tradition is gaining momentum, and on February 9, 2014, country cleanup leaders from around the world agreed to the goal of involving 380 million people by 2018.

Question 1 of 6
The passage suggests that the main goal of the cleanup days was to encourage people to

Answers	
A	spend more time in nature
B	volunteer for meaningful causes
C	commit to making a cleaner planet
D	travel to neighboring countries

First, find the question topic: this question asks about the **specific** idea of *cleanup days* and what they encouraged people to do.

Now, read the passage to find what it has to say about that topic. If you want to be a little aggressive, you could stop reading as soon as you see "cleanup days" in the second sentence; this phrase immediately follows the previous sentence, which describes a *worldwide movement to combat the global solid waste problem*.

You now have your **evidence**, so you can start eliminating choices.

> **Choices A** and **B** are both true but irrelevant based on what the passage says—the cleanup days do allow people to spend time in *nature* for a *meaningful cause*—but neither of them is the **main goal** of the cleanup days.

> **Choice D** is also incorrect because the passage never really discusses *traveling to neighboring countries*, so this idea is totally **unrelated** to the question.

> **Choice C** is the best answer because *commit to making a cleaner planet* is very similar to our evidence, *combat the global solid waste problem*.

NOTES:

_____

_____

_____

This page is intentionally left blank.

Try the strategy on the following question:

The red oak, the black oak, and the scarlet oak—all splendid forest trees of the Northeast—are in the group of confusion that can be readily separated only by the timber-cruiser, who knows every tree in the forest for its economic value, or by the botanist, with his paperback Gray's Manual in hand. I confess to bewilderment in five minutes after the differences have been explained to me, and I enjoyed, not long ago, the confusion of a skillful nurseryman who was endeavoring to show me his young trees of red oak that the label proved to be scarlet!

Which of the following best describes what "timber-cruiser" means as it is used in the passage?

A	A casual lover of nature who uses a guidebook for reference
B	A botanist or scientist who has extensive knowledge of trees
C	An individual who assesses the worth of trees for profit
D	A nurseryman who must assign names to and label young trees

NOTES:

_____

_____

_____

_____

_____

_____

_____

_____

This time, the question wants to know about a *timber-cruiser*, which is mentioned in the first sentence. Our evidence is the phrase *who knows every tree in the forest for its economic value*. The only choice that matches our evidence is choice C, which specifically states *profit*, a concept related to *economic value*.

NOTES:

_____

_____

_____

_____

_____

_____

_____

_____

_____

_____

_____

_____

_____

_____

Get the Main Idea

It's a little harder to find evidence when a question asks for the **main idea** or **main purpose** of a passage. In these cases, the evidence is the **entire passage**. The best way to handle these questions is to create a good summary of what you read before eliminating answer choices.

Take a look at the second question from the exercise:

Passage
When we think of blushing, embarrassment, redness, and a rise in temperature come to mind—all noticeable in the face. Most people are surprised to discover the phenomenon of blushing also occurs in the stomach. Because adrenaline causes tiny blood vessels called capillaries to widen and increase blood flow, the tissue around these vessels in the stomach appears as red as a blushing cheek. Though this may seem unnatural to some, the stomach is just another example of how the brain uses chemical processes to prepare the body for fight or flight in often unnoticed ways.

Question 2 of 6
The main idea of the passage is that

	Answers
A	blushing in the face is identical to blushing in the stomach
B	adrenaline causes blood vessels to widen for increased blood flow
C	the stomach is the most prepared part of the body for fight or flight
D	stomach blushing goes unnoticed but is a natural process

Since the question asks for the *main idea* of the passage, you will need to read and summarize the entire thing. The key is to think about how all the sentences work together to form a main idea.

In this case, the **first sentence** introduces the idea of *blushing*. The **second sentence** points out how people are *surprised* to find out that *blushing also occurs in the stomach*. The **third** and **fourth** sentences provide some explanation of this process and how it relates to the *fight or flight* phenomenon.

Putting it all together, we can summarize this passage to something like the following:

Though most people don't know it, the stomach also blushes as a result of adrenaline that is released into the body in preparation for fight or flight.

This is obviously going to be a lot longer than the correct answer, but it gives a baseline for tackling the choice. Now, on to elimination.

Choices A and **B** are attractive because they are both stated directly in the passage, but they are **too narrow**: choice A does not address the end of the passage, and choice B only covers the third sentence.

Choice C is incorrect for a few reasons, but mostly because it is **too extreme**. Although the passage states that the stomach is prepared for fight or flight, it does not say that it is the *most prepared*.

Choice D is the correct answer because it accurately sums up the **entire** passage.

This page is intentionally left blank.

Give it a try on the following passage:

Presidential transitions, the transfer of power from the current U.S. president to the newly elected president, used to be straightforward, but now they include several requirements such as replacing cabinet members, developing a review team, and creating a policy agenda. The Presidential Transition Act of 1963 made the process for presidential transitions more official (specifically assigning a transition team and providing funds for the process). The Presidential Transitions Effectiveness Act of 1998 increased the amount of money toward this cause, and the Presidential Transition Act of 2000 further expanded it to include resources for training incoming appointees who would be filling key positions.

What is the main purpose of this passage?

A	To explain the need for a presidential transition process
B	To describe how presidential transition processes have been applied
C	To show how the presidential transition process has developed
D	To argue that the presidential transition process needs to be revised

NOTES:

This time, the question is asking for the **main purpose**. This is one step away from **main idea**, since it is asking *why* the author wrote the passage instead of *what* the author wanted to say.

The strategy is the same, however. Start with your summary and then eliminate answers that don't match. In this case, your summary should look like this:

> *The process of changing from one president to the next has gotten much more complex over time, partly as the result of several acts, which also provided more resources for the change.*

The answers will not match our summary because the question is looking for the **purpose** behind the passage. However, you can still use this summary to eliminate choices that do not fit. Then you can compare what's left and make an educated guess.

> **Choices A** and **D** are incorrect because they introduce ideas—the need for the process and the argument that it needs additional revision—that are **not discussed** anywhere in our summary or in the passage.

> To decide between **choice B**, which focuses on the *application* of the process, and **choice C**, which focuses on the *development* of the process, you can ask: which of these topics is discussed the *most* in the passage?

In this case, we see descriptions of several acts that changed the transition process, so the idea of changing, or *developing*, best fits the purpose, making choice C the correct answer.

NOTES:

_____

_____

_____

_____

_____

_____

_____

_____

DRAWING CONCLUSIONS

When a question asks you to *infer* or *draw a conclusion* from the passage, you are being asked to make **an inference**. You should keep a few things in mind when this happens:

- An inference is a conclusion based on **evidence**.
- All inferences can be directly **supported by the passage**.
- It is **impossible** for an inference to be "too close" to the passage text.
- Watch out for **assumptions**—try to use the author's words as evidence instead of your interpretation.

Look at the third question from the exercise:

Passage
I can still smell the rich aroma of our olive oil. There were so many flavors in it: spicy pepper, the green earthiness of tomato leaves, and a light, banana-like sweetness behind it all. My *nonna* would use it in her marinara and drizzle it on top of gnocchi with parmesan, and it tasted like heaven. It satisfied the palate in a way nothing else could.

Question 3 of 6
Which of the following conclusions about the narrator's response to the aroma can most logically be drawn from the passage?

Answers	
A	She is disappointed over a painful loss.
B	She is delighted by the warmth of a pleasant memory.
C	She is saddened that she is not still living on the family farm.
D	She is filled with satisfaction from completing a difficult task.

Notice that the question wants you to draw a conclusion about the *narrator's response to the aroma*. Look in the passage and find how she responds. Remember to stick closely to what the author has to say instead of your own take on it.

The passage describes the smell of olive oil used by her *nonna* and specifically says that it *tasted like heaven*. Use that to eliminate answers that don't match.

Choices A and **C** are incorrect because *disappoint, painful loss,* and *saddened* **don't match** the positive language in the passage.

Choice D is incorrect because the author **never discusses** or implies a *difficult task* was completed.

Choice B is correct because *delighted* and *pleasant memory* fit with the positive description in the passage.

This page is intentionally left blank.

Try drawing a conclusion from the following passage:

Despite the rough sound quality, the general public was captivated by recorded music. The Pacific Phonograph Company installed the first coin-operated phonograph in a San Francisco saloon in 1889, which allowed people to select and listen to a song for one nickel. This early jukebox was extremely popular, and by the mid-1890s most American cities had at least one "phonograph parlor." A few years later, these machines were more reasonably priced and could be found in many homes. This was followed by an increase of sales in phonograph wax cylinders (which were used to record the music itself).

Which of the following conclusions about the popularity of "phonograph parlors" in the 1890s can most reasonably be drawn from the passage?

A	They made recorded music seem practically worthless, since each play only cost a nickel.
B	They resulted in less work for live music performers.
C	They led to the development of afford-able phonographs for the home.
D	They demanded a stronger recording device than wax cylinders.

NOTES:

_____

_____

_____

_____

_____

_____

_____

The topic of the question this time is *the popularity of "phonograph parlors" in the 1890s*. Unfortunately, almost the entire passage covers this topic. This type of question is called a **general inference**, meaning we can't point to one specific part of the passage before looking at the answers.

In this case, the best tactic is to **work backward** by looking at each choice and determining if you can find some evidence in the passage.

> **Choice A** states that the music seemed *practically worthless* because each play only cost a nickel. This is an example of an **assumption**, as the passage never told us that people thought the songs were worthless due to the cost. Eliminate choice A.

> **Choice B** discusses *live music performers*, which is never mentioned in the passage at all, so this too can be eliminated.

> **Choice C** mentions *affordable phonographs*, which fits well with *these machines* being *more reasonably priced* in the fourth sentence, so keep it for now.

> **Choice D** introduces the idea of the strength of wax cylinders. While wax cylinders are discussed in relation to phonographs, it does not discuss their *strength* at any point, making this choice **half right**. Eliminate choice D.

Only choice C fits with a topic discussed in the passage, so it is the correct answer.

NOTES:

_____

_____

_____

_____

_____

_____

_____

_____

Short Passage, Practice Set Two

Passage

A principal reason for the decline of singing in modern times is that the tuning of pitch has gradually and considerably risen during the last 150 years. As orchestras increasingly tune at higher frequencies, the vocal apparatus has been unable to bear the strain to which it is now subjected. With regard to tenors, however, the greater evil is that they disregard the falsetto register, singing everything, however high, in chest voice. Certainly they have not been beguiled into this serious mistake by the faint rise of tuning pitch just mentioned. The truth is that they have committed this fatal blunder knowingly and willfully—because they saw that it was more exciting to the public and knew it would draw in larger audiences.

Question 4 of 6

Based on the passage, the rise of tuning pitch in music occurred

Answers

A	only in modern times
B	mainly due to the falsetto register
C	in the past two centuries
D	with the invention of a new apparatus

Passage

A narcissist is someone with obsessive admiration for the self and who shows a need for excessive attention or praise. The name comes from a tale in Greek mythology in which Narcissus, a hunter known for his beauty, became so attracted to his reflection in a pool of water he fell in love. However, when the object of his affection could not love him back, Narcissus became distraught and withered away, leaving behind a narcissus flower.

Question 5 of 6

What is the overall purpose of the passage?

Answers

A	To recount a tale from Greek mythology
B	To describe the origin of a word
C	To stress the need to be cautious in love
D	To demonstrate the difficulties of finding love

Passage

BN Vocational School was established in 2005 to address a prevalent problem in China's state-run vocation schools: inadequately trained graduates whose severe knowledge gaps result in poor job performance. Today, nine campuses are scattered across the country, offering tailor-made courses that place graduates directly into employment in their geographical region. "In Dalian, mechanical operations has the largest class," says Qiang Liu, spokesperson for the BNVS campus network, referring to the highly industrialized city in the north. "Whereas in Sanya," situated on a tropical island in the South China Sea, "most students enroll in air-conditioning operation and maintenance." The full curriculum available at various BNVS campuses includes hotel management, tourism, web production, and graphic design—a first in China's history. They even offer a dozen or so "long-term development courses," such as financial literacy, philanthropy, and English.

The passage indicates that BN Vocational School adapted the curriculums of its various campuses in order to

Answers

A	match graduates' skills with the demands of local industry
B	give students more options in what they are able to study
C	not compete with other regional trade schools
D	meet government regulations

SECTION TWO, ELAR:
LONG PASSAGE

LONG PASSAGE, PRACTICE SET ONE

Passage

In this passage from a biography, the writer describes one man's journey to develop a career as a modern-day philosopher.

Daniel Dennett's eternal search for answers began after his father was killed in an unexplained plane crash. His early life and move from Beirut to Massachusetts was cast in the long shadow of a mythical, unknown father figure. Dennett had come from a family of remarkable brilliance—his father was a counter-intelligence officer in the Office of Strategic Services, a predecessor of the CIA. Dennett attended Harvard University, where he received a doctorate in philosophy. There he was awarded the prestigious Erasmus prize for his exceptional contribution to society, showcasing how his work was not only important to himself but was also significant within a worldwide community.

During Dennett's first year at Winchester High School, he put all his effort into a term paper on Plato and included a picture of Rodin's *The Thinker* on the cover. He humorously recalled that at the time, he hadn't really understood a word of what he had written. At age seventeen he had begun pursuing a mathematics degree at Wesleyan University and found himself drowning in his coursework. Studying in the library late one evening, he chanced upon the text *From a Logical Point of View*, which had been written at Harvard University by Willard Van Orman Quine. He was utterly transfixed, and by the next morning he had made up his mind to transfer to Harvard.

At the end of his college career, Dennett had begun developing his own thoughts and contradicting the opinions of philosophers who came before him. By 1962 he was twenty and married and could no longer relate to the idyllic days of his youth. He was experiencing for the first time a voracious drive to refute Quine's work. His youthful misguidance had now

Passage (cont.)

been given purpose. He chose to follow the path of questioning established truths, and regardless of the daunting complexities involved, he was coming up with His Own Answers. Now there was no turning back; he was the one calling the shots. In his thesis defense, he was so convincing that an established professor defended one of his critiques of Quine against the objections of another faculty member. This remarkable affirmation inspired in him true self-confidence, and Dennett went on to build an academic career asking poignant questions.

Question 1 of 6

The main purpose of the passage is to

Answers

A	propose that by following the steps taken by Dennett, others can become philosophers as well
B	persuade the reader that Dennett was only able to ask questions no one could answer
C	speculate on how philosophers employ different methods to approach an argument
D	describe how Dennett developed from an inexperienced student into an established philosopher

Question 2 of 6
The author capitalizes the words in the third paragraph most likely to signify that

Answers	
A	Dennett believed that only his opinions were valid
B	these are Quine's words, not Dennett's
C	Dennett had begun to form theories of his own
D	Dennett and Quine no longer respected one another

Question 3 of 6
The third paragraph suggests that Dennett saw philosophy as

Answers	
A	a subject that is less valuable than science
B	a hobby not worth investing in
C	a useless but interesting subject
D	a challenging but fulfilling area of study

THE LONG PASSAGE BASIC STRATEGY

All **Long Passages** on the TSIA2 ELAR test have the same basic characteristics, which will help us develop our strategy.

- The passage will be about three to four times **longer than a short passage**.
- The passage will have **exactly 3 questions**.
- The passage will tell a **story**.

THE BASIC STRATEGY

1. **Read the Passage First**
   You can look at the first question to see what it has to say, but you can't preview all of the questions because of how the TSIA2 is organized. It is usually best to just jump right into the passage.

2. **Find the Big Picture**
   The best way to get the big picture is to jot down **one idea per paragraph**. Then, string the ideas together into a **summary** of the entire passage.

3. **Read the Question**
   If you didn't preview the question already, or you are on the second or third question, read the question now to determine the **topic** and **where** you need to look for your evidence.

4. **Find Your Evidence**
   This step is the same as it is on any Reading question. Find your evidence either **directly** in the passage or in your **summary**.

5. **Use the Process of Elimination**
   Eliminate as many answers as you can right away. Then, compare what's left and choose the best remaining option. Remember to watch out for common trap answers!

NOTES:

_____

_____

_____

_____

_____

Let's give the strategy a try on question one in the exercise. First, take a look at the passage and summarize it by getting the main idea of each paragraph:

Paragraph One: Dennett came from an intelligent, accomplished family, and he was also very talented.

Paragraph Two: Dennett struggled in school but was inspired to transfer to Harvard.

Paragraph Three: Dennett began to think for himself and built a career out of it.

Summary: Dennett was a smart young man who developed into a brilliant thinker after struggling in his early years.

You don't necessarily need to write it down, but you should at least take the time to **understand and summarize** the passage in your head as you read. **Don't worry** about the small details, especially if you are confused by them. Just get the big picture at first.

Next, look at the question: since this question is asking for the **main purpose**, we should use our summary as much as possible. Let's start eliminating answers:

Choices A and **C** are incorrect because they are both **off topic**. They talk about *other philosophers*, but our summary is focused only on Dennett.

Choice B is incorrect because it is **too extreme** in saying Dennett was *only able to ask questions no one could answer,* which is not supported by the passage.

Choice D is the correct answer because the statement *Dennett developed from an inexperienced student into an established philosopher* is very similar to our summary.

NOTES:

_____

_____

_____

_____

_____

_____

This page is intentionally left blank.

Give this strategy a try on the following question:

In this passage from a biography, the writer describes one man's journey to develop a career as a modern-day philosopher.

Daniel Dennett's eternal search for answers began after his father was killed in an unexplained plane crash. His early life and move from Beirut to Massachusetts was cast in the long shadow of a mythical, unknown father figure. Dennett had come from a family of remarkable brilliance—his father was a counter-intelligence officer in the Office of Strategic Services, a predecessor of the CIA. Dennett attended Harvard University, where he received a doctorate in philosophy. There he was awarded the prestigious Erasmus prize for his exceptional contribution to society, showcasing how his work was not only important to himself but was also significant within a worldwide community.

During Dennett's first year at Winchester High School, he put all his effort into a term paper on Plato and included a picture of Rodin's *The Thinker* on the cover. He humorously recalled that at the time, he hadn't really understood a word of what he had written. At age seventeen he had begun pursuing a mathematics degree at Wesleyan University and found himself drowning in his coursework. Studying in the library late one evening, he chanced upon the text *From a Logical Point of View*, which had been written at Harvard University by Willard Van Orman Quine. He was utterly transfixed, and by the next morning he had made up his mind to transfer to Harvard.

At the end of his college career, Dennett had begun developing his own thoughts and contradicting the opinions of philosophers who came before him. By 1962 he was twenty and married and could no longer relate to the idyllic days of his youth. He was experiencing for the first time a voracious drive to refute Quine's work. His youthful misguidance had now

been given purpose. He chose to follow the path of questioning established truths, and regardless of the daunting complexities involved, he was coming up with His Own Answers. Now there was no turning back; he was the one calling the shots. In his thesis defense, he was so convincing that an established professor defended one of his critiques of Quine against the objections of another faculty member. This remarkable affirmation inspired in him true self-confidence, and Dennett went on to build an academic career asking poignant questions.

The main purpose of the second paragraph is to

A	describe a specific text written by Dennett's rival, Quine
B	present the process students undertake to defend their philosophical theses
C	provide an account of Dennett's transformation from youth to maturity
D	list several ways Dennett contradicted the teachings of his mentors

This question is similar in that it focuses on the **main purpose**—this time, for a specific paragraph—and not on a specific detail. Since we have already summarized the second paragraph, we are ready to start eliminating answers.

Choices **A** and **B** are incorrect because they are **too narrow**, each focusing on a specific detail in the paragraph and not the **main** purpose.

Choice D is incorrect because the paragraph never discusses *mentors*.

Choice C is the correct answer because the idea of transitioning from *youth to maturity* matches our summary of Dennett struggling in school before being inspired to change schools and switch majors.

NOTES:

_____

_____

_____

_____

_____

_____

_____

_____

_____

_____

FINDING MEANING

Some questions on the TSIA2 will be so **specific**, they will ask for the meaning or purpose of specific phrases or even words. In this case, you will need to find the specific words or phrases in the passage and use the **context and meaning** to help you decide on the best answer.

Take a look at question two from the exercise:

Question 2 of 6
The author capitalizes the words in the third paragraph most likely to signify that

Answers	
A	Dennett believed that only his opinions were valid
B	these are Quine's words, not Dennett's
C	Dennett had begun to form theories of his own
D	Dennett and Quine no longer respected one another

The question wants you to look at the words that are capitalized in the third paragraph: *he was coming up with His Own Answers.*

Before jumping to eliminating answers, take a minute to **understand** what is going on in this part of the passage. At this point, Dennett has finally started to develop his *own thoughts*. The passage even says that he *was the one calling the shots*. We can safely conclude that the author capitalized the words *His Own Answers* to reflect this **context**.

Now we are ready to eliminate.

> **Choices A** and **D** are incorrect because they are **too extreme**. The author isn't saying that Dennett thought *only his opinions were valid*, and it is too much of an **assumption** to say Quine and Dennett did not respect one another.

> **Choice B** is incorrect because it states the **opposite** of the passage. Remember that the context is all about how *Dennett* is now in charge, so it would not make sense if Quine were the one speaking at that point.

> **Choice C** is correct because the idea that Dennett was creating *theories of his own* is right in line with the capitalized words as well as the context of the paragraph.

This page is intentionally left blank.

Consider the following example and keep the strategy in mind:

In this passage from a novel, the writer describes one man's journey to develop a career as a modern-day philosopher.

Daniel Dennett's eternal search for answers began after his father was killed in an unexplained plane crash. His early life and move from Beirut to Massachusetts was cast in the long shadow of a mythical, unknown father figure. Dennett had come from a family of remarkable brilliance—his father was a counter-intelligence officer in the Office of Strategic Services, a predecessor of the CIA. Dennett attended Harvard University, where he received a doctorate in philosophy. There he was awarded the prestigious Erasmus prize for his exceptional contribution to society, showcasing how his work was not only important to himself but was also significant within a worldwide community.

During Dennett's first year at Winchester High School, he put all his effort into a term paper on Plato and included a picture of Rodin's *The Thinker* on the cover. He humorously recalled that at the time, he hadn't really understood a word of what he had written. At age seventeen he had begun pursuing a mathematics degree at Wesleyan University and found himself drowning in his coursework. Studying in the library late one evening, he chanced upon the text *From a Logical Point of View*, which had been written at Harvard University by Willard Van Orman Quine. He was utterly transfixed, and by the next morning he had made up his mind to transfer to Harvard.

At the end of his college career, Dennett had begun developing his own thoughts and contradicting the opinions of philosophers who came before him. By 1962 he was twenty and married and could no longer relate to the idyllic days of his youth. He was experiencing for the first time a voracious drive to refute Quine's work. His youthful misguidance had now

been given purpose. He chose to follow the path of questioning established truths, and regardless of the daunting complexities involved, he was coming up with His Own Answers. Now there was no turning back; he was the one calling the shots. In his thesis defense, he was so convincing that an established professor defended one of his critiques of Quine against the objections of another faculty member. This remarkable affirmation inspired in him true self-confidence, and Dennett went on to build an academic career asking poignant questions.

The details describing Dennett's father in the first paragraph are most likely included to

A	explain that Dennett felt an urge to follow in his father's footsteps
B	demonstrate the legacy of intelligence Dennett was born into
C	suggest that Dennett's father's military career was similar to that of Dennett's in academia
D	show that few philosophers relate to growing up in a military household

This time, the question wants to know how specific details are used in the first paragraph. Go back to the first paragraph to find the details and then determine the **context**.

The first paragraph focuses on Dennett's **extraordinary background**, and the specific details focus on how his father is an example of his **brilliant family**. We have our evidence, so we can start eliminating.

Choice A is incorrect because it makes an **assumption.** While we know Dennett's father was brilliant, there is no evidence that Dennett wanted to follow after his father.

Choice C is incorrect because it draws a **false comparison**. The passage never implies that Dennett's father had a career that was similar to Dennett's career.

Choice D is incorrect because the first paragraph does not talk about other philosophers.

Choice B is the correct answer because it points out the *legacy of intelligence* of Dennett's family and background, which **matches** our evidence.

NOTES:

_____

_____

_____

_____

_____

_____

_____

_____

_____

POINT OF VIEW

Long passages will often present **multiple points of view** throughout the passage, so it is important that you keep them straight if a question asks about a particular viewpoint.

- Pay attention to alternative viewpoints and expect to see them as **trap answers**.
- Don't confuse the **author's** point of view with the point of view referred to in the **question**.
- It helps to jot down the different points of view during your **summary**.

Take a look at question three from the exercise:

Question 3 of 6
The third paragraph suggests that Dennett saw philosophy as

Answers	
A	a subject that is less valuable than science
B	a hobby not worth investing in
C	a useless but interesting subject
D	a challenging but fulfilling area of study

The question asks about **Dennett's point of view**, specifically how he sees philosophy as described in the third paragraph. The passage describes how he found himself by challenging past philosophers and how he found *true self-confidence*.

Choices **A**, **B**, and **C** can all be eliminated because they are **opposite** the right answer. Each one says a negative thing about the *worth* of philosophy—*less valuable, not worth investing in,* and *useless*—when we know that Dennett finds philosophy extremely valuable.

Choice **D** is correct because *challenging* **matches** the phrase *daunting complexities* in the third paragraph and because we know Dennett found philosophy to be satisfying.

This page is intentionally left blank.

Try out a slightly different version of a point of view question below:

In this passage from a biography, the writer describes one man's journey to develop a career as a modern-day philosopher.

Daniel Dennett's eternal search for answers began after his father was killed in an unexplained plane crash. His early life and move from Beirut to Massachusetts was cast in the long shadow of a mythical, unknown father figure. Dennett had come from a family of remarkable brilliance—his father was a counter-intelligence officer in the Office of Strategic Services, a predecessor of the CIA. Dennett attended Harvard University, where he received a doctorate in philosophy. There he was awarded the prestigious Erasmus prize for his exceptional contribution to society, showcasing how his work was not only important to himself but was also significant within a worldwide community.

During Dennett's first year at Winchester High School, he put all his effort into a term paper on Plato and included a picture of Rodin's *The Thinker* on the cover. He humorously recalled that at the time, he hadn't really understood a word of what he had written. At age seventeen he had begun pursuing a mathematics degree at Wesleyan University and found himself drowning in his coursework. Studying in the library late one evening, he chanced upon the text *From a Logical Point of View*, which had been written at Harvard University by Willard Van Orman Quine. He was utterly transfixed, and by the next morning he had made up his mind to transfer to Harvard.

At the end of his college career, Dennett had begun developing his own thoughts and contradicting the opinions of philosophers who came before him. By 1962 he was twenty and married and could no longer relate to the idyllic days of his youth. He was experiencing for the first time a voracious drive to refute Quine's work. His youthful misguidance had now

been given purpose. He chose to follow the path of questioning established truths, and regardless of the daunting complexities involved, he was coming up with His Own Answers. Now there was no turning back; he was the one calling the shots. In his thesis defense, he was so convincing that an established professor defended one of his critiques of Quine against the objections of another faculty member. This remarkable affirmation inspired in him true self-confidence, and Dennett went on to build an academic career asking poignant questions.

Details in the passage suggest that the narrator is

A	an author describing the life of a passionate person
B	a philosopher recalling the memory of a friend
C	a son remembering his father's death
D	a parent recalling his college years

Since this question asks about the *narrator,* you will need to use your **summary** as a starting point for your eliminations.

> **Choice B** is incorrect because even though the passage is about a philosopher, the **point of view** is from someone who is *describing* the philosopher.

> **Choices C** and **D** are incorrect because while the passage does discuss a *son* and a *parent*, the passage is not from their **point of view**.

> **Choice A** is correct because it simply describes the narrator as **an author** who is detailing the *life of a passionate person*, specifically, Dennett.

NOTES:

_____

_____

_____

_____

_____

_____

_____

_____

_____

_____

_____

This page is intentionally left blank.

LONG PASSAGE, PRACTICE SET TWO

Passage

The narrator of this passage, excerpted from an essay, describes the life of a pet dog.

The day he came was a beautiful, bright, cool one in August. A touring car brought him. They put him down on our corner, meaning to lose him, but he crawled under the car, and they had to prod him out and throw stones before they could drive on. I carried him over the railroad tracks. That night he got chop bones and slept on the mat. The second morning we thought he had gone. The third he was back, wagging approval of us and intent to stay, which seemed to leave no choice but to take him in. We had fun over names: "Jellywaggles," "Rags," or "Toby." Finally we called him "Nibbie," and soon his tail would answer to it.

Cleaned up—scrubbed, the insoluble matted locks clipped from his coat, his trampish collar replaced with a new one bearing a license tag—he was far from being unpresentable. Always, depending on the moment's mood, he was either terrier or spaniel, the snap and scrap and perk of the one alternating with the gentle snuggling indolence of the other.

As terrier he would dig furiously by the hour after a field mouse; as spaniel he would "read" the breeze with the best nose among the dog folk of our neighborhood or follow a trail quite well. I know there was retrieving blood. A year ago in May he caught and brought me, not doing the least injury, an oriole that probably had flown against a wire and was struggling disabled in the grass.

Nibbie was shabby-genteel black, sunburnt as to the mustache, grizzled as to the raggy fringe on his haunches. He had a white stock and shirt frill and a white forepaw. The brown eyes full of heart were the best point. His body coat was rough Scottish worsted, the little black pate was cotton-soft like shoddy, and the big black ears

Passage (cont.)

were genuine spaniel silk. As a terrier he held them up smartly and carried a plumy fishhook of a tail; as a spaniel the ears drooped and the tail swung meekly as if in apology for never having been clipped. In flea time it seemed hardly possible that a dog of his size could sustain his population. We finally found a true flea bane, but deserted one day, he was populous again the next.

Question 4 of 6

In describing Nibbie's problem with fleas and the doubt that Nibbie could "sustain his population," the narrator is most directly referring to the fact that

Answers

A	the fleas living on Nibbie made him afraid to leave the clothes-closet to eat his dinner
B	Nibbie wagged his tail at the family but snapped blindly at fleas when left alone
C	no other dog in the neighborhood had as many fleas as Nibbie had that season
D	the large number of fleas living on Nibbie was incongruous to his small size

Question 5 of 6
When the author says that Nibbie's first owners let him out "meaning to lose him," he most likely means

Answers	
A	the first owners were careless and could not keep track of him
B	Nibbie's owners were abandoning him
C	Nibbie wandered off and got lost
D	the author lost Nibbie under the car

Question 6 of 6
When the author writes that Nibbie had "retrieving blood," he most likely means that he

Answers	
A	was a ferocious hunter that brought back his kills to the narrator
B	had a health problem involving his blood vessels
C	sustained a gruesome injury while playing fetch
D	displayed characteristics of a particular breed of dog

Section Two, ELAR:
Dual Passage

Dual Passage, Practice Set One

Passage

Passage 1

Should time-consuming athletic programs be cut from schools? Ongoing research indicates the opposite. One study looked at various factors indicating health and social values of both student athletes and their non-sport-playing peers. Researchers found that young people who play competitive sports tend to have a higher GPA and spend more hours studying than students who don't play sports. Additionally, rates of depression and anxiety are lower for student athletes than for their non-sport counterparts. Researchers also learned student athletes are more likely to have an active, healthy lifestyle as they grow older than those who did not participate in sports. Already familiar with exercising, goal setting, and pushing through challenges, teen athletes can carry these habits into adulthood.

Passage 2

Playing defense on my high school's soccer team, I admit it's hard to focus on whatever is going on in class when it's game day. Practice days can be pretty grueling—we spend hours either in exhausting drills or in mandatory study hall to keep our GPA up. Before I played sports, I got more rest, and I had friends from different organizations around school. I knew other students because we rode the bus together or were in the same group for a science project. Now, I spend most of my time at practice, and since my teammates are my friends, it's natural to spend our free time together, too. Then again, what's free time?

Question 1 of 4

What would the author of Passage 2 most likely say is the cause of the "more hours" (Passage 1, sentence 4) student athletes spend studying?

Answers

A	The injuries caused by accidents during practice
B	The difficulty of completing homework with limited free time
C	The interruption to class due to traveling to away games
D	The requirement to maintain a high GPA

Question 2 of 4

The authors of both passages would probably characterize student athletes as being generally

Answers

A	overwhelmed
B	healthy
C	friendless
D	satisfied

THE DUAL PASSAGE BASIC STRATEGY

Dual Passages always consist of exactly two short passages, one paragraph each, and either one or two questions. The questions ask about how these passages **relate** or how they **differ**.

THE BASIC STRATEGY

1. **Read the Question First**
    It is common to only have **one question**, so you should treat the question the same as with a **short passage**.

    Determine the following:

    -   **Topic:** What is the question asking about?
    -   **Relationship:** How do the two passages relate to the question?

    For example, is the question asking how the passages **agree** or **disagree?** Is it asking you to find a topic in Passage 1 but **not** in Passage 2?

2. **Read Passage 1 and Eliminate if You Can**
    If the question is **specific** enough, you can read Passage 1 to find what you need and start eliminating choices if possible.

    If the question is more **general**, just read and summarize Passage 1 the way you would for **short passages.**

3. **Repeat for Passage 2**
    Read Passage 2. If you couldn't eliminate any answer choices after reading Passage 1, you should be able to **start eliminating** now.

    If you still can't make eliminations, create your **summary**.

4. **Compare and Contrast the Passages**
    If the question is more general, you will need to compare and contrast the passages before you can answer the question.

    Consider the following:

    -   What are the **topics** of both passages?
    -   How do the authors **agree** on that topic?
    -   How do the authors **disagree** on that topic?

5. **Use the Process of Elimination**
    Reread the question and start eliminating choices that don't fit. On **Dual Passages**, you should specifically look for the following common traps:

    -   **Half right:** These are answer choices that describe one passage correctly but get the other one wrong.
    -   **Opposite:** These are answer choices that reverse the opinions of the two passages.

Look at question one from the exercise:

Question 1 of 4
What would the author of Passage 2 most likely say is the cause of the "more hours" (Passage 1, sentence 4) student athletes spend studying?

	Answers
A	The injuries caused by accidents during practice
B	The difficulty of completing homework with limited free time
C	The interruption to class due to traveling to away games
D	The requirement to maintain a high GPA

First, read the question and determine the **topic** and how **each passage** relates to it.

Since we need to know a lot about both passages, we won't be able to eliminate anything until we read and **summarize** the passages.

> **Passage 1:** Despite some commonly held beliefs, athletic programs create excellent students who benefit from athletics in a number of ways.

> **Passage 2:** A particular student athlete struggles with the balance between athletics and studying and finds that they often oppose each other.

Since the question asks how **Passage 2** would explain the **cause of *more hours*** studying, mentioned specifically in **Passage 1**, we know the perspective will be from a student athlete who is struggling with school. With that in mind, let's start eliminating answer choices:

> **Choices A** and **C** are wrong because they **assume** the student athlete's *grueling practice* creates injuries or that the student is distracted on game day because she will be traveling to an away game.

> **Choice B** is incorrect because the student athlete never really discusses homework.

> **Choice D** is correct because Passage 2 emphasizes *mandatory study hall* and keeping up a GPA, which is a good reason to explain additional studying hours.

Try the basic strategy again with the following passage set and question:

Passage 1

I recently met a ninth-grade teacher who told me over half of her students drank coffee in the mornings. Some of her students said they started drinking coffee as early as sixth grade. Others said they only started in high school—where the gym vending machine sells cold coffee drinks. A handful of the non-coffee drinkers admitted they drink caffeinated soda to wake up every morning. As a matter of fact, about 64% of Americans have a cup of coffee every morning rather than waking up naturally. This is a shame! Now more than ever, people need to return to more natural ways of living—especially young, developing children. Parents, end your children's caffeine consumption and ensure they get enough sleep every night instead!

Passage 2

There are almost no conclusive statistics about the number of young people consuming caffeine daily. Fatigued students struggle to focus in class and perform poorly on tests, however, and many other nations with a culture of tea-drinking consistently have higher-scoring students than the United States. It's possible that American students are not as alert and productive as their caffeinated counterparts. Coffee and tea also contain antioxidants and some essential nutrients, so caffeinated drinks can provide a variety of benefits, from improved physical health to mental stimulation and clarity. Obviously, it is logical for parents to allow their children to consume caffeine, including coffee, in the morning for their well-being.

The author of Passage 2 would probably respond to the last sentence of Passage 1 ("Parents...night instead!") by

A	emphasizing that parents should help children balance rest and caffeine consumption
B	pointing out that children consume more caffeine at a young age than their parents did
C	asserting that children prefer the taste of coffee over water or juice
D	arguing that children should be drinking more coffee in the mornings

NOTES:

_____

_____

_____

The two passages disagree on whether young people should consume more caffeine, specifically in the form of coffee. **Passage 1** thinks it is a *bad idea*. **Passage 2** thinks it is a *great idea*.

The question wants to know how Passage 2 would respond to Passage 1's statement that parents should end their *children's caffeine consumption*. Since we know that Passage 2 is **pro-coffee**, we are ready to eliminate some answer choices:

> **Choice A** can be eliminated because the author of Passage 2 is in favor of more caffeine consumption, so she would not suggest a balance.

> **Choices B** and **C** are incorrect because they each introduce **irrelevant** subjects, specifically comparing children to parents in choice B and comparing the taste of water and juice in choice C.

> **Choice D** is correct because it lines up almost exactly with our summary for Passage 2.

NOTES:

_____

_____

_____

_____

_____

_____

_____

_____

_____

_____

AGREE TO DISAGREE

The core skill you need for **Dual Passage** questions is the ability to find how the passages **agree** and **disagree**. Keep the following points in mind:

- **Always** mark whether the question is looking for an **agreement** or a **disagreement** before you start eliminating answers.
- Be on the lookout for the **opposite** trap answer.

Consider question two from the exercise:

Question 2 of 4
The authors of both passages would probably characterize student athletes as being generally

	Answers
A	overwhelmed
B	healthy
C	friendless
D	satisfied

This question asks for a point of **agreement** between the two passages. If you look at your summary, you will see that these two passages are strongly opposed to each other. Since our summary won't be specific enough to help us see how they agree, we will need to work backward from the answer choices.

Choice A states *overwhelmed*, which would be supported by the narrator of Passage 2, who says, *what's free time?* But the author of Passage 1 does not mention student athletes being overwhelmed, so eliminate it.

Choice B states *healthy*, which both passages attribute to student athletes, so keep this choice.

Choice C states *friendless*, which contradicts the claim in Passage 2 that the author spends time with friends from the team, so eliminate it.

Choice D states *satisfied*, but Passage 1 does not make this claim, and Passage 2 expresses more of the negative aspects of being a student athlete, so it can also be eliminated.

This leaves choice B as the correct answer.

This page is intentionally left blank.

Give it a try on the passage from earlier:

Passage 1

I recently met a ninth-grade teacher who told me over half of her students drank coffee in the mornings. Some of her students said they started drinking coffee as early as sixth grade. Others said they only started in high school—where the gym vending machine sells cold coffee drinks. A handful of the non-coffee drinkers admitted they drink caffeinated soda to wake up every morning. As a matter of fact, about 64% of Americans have a cup of coffee every morning rather than waking up naturally. This is a shame! Now more than ever, people need to return to more natural ways of living— especially young, developing children. Parents, end your children's caffeine consumption and ensure they get enough sleep every night instead!

Passage 2

There are almost no conclusive statistics about the number of young people consuming caffeine daily. Fatigued students struggle to focus in class and perform poorly on tests, however, and many other nations with a culture of tea-drinking consistently have higher-scoring students than the United States. It's possible that American students are not as alert and productive as their caffeinated counterparts. Coffee and tea also contain antioxidants and some essential nutrients, so caffeinated drinks can provide a variety of benefits, from physical health benefits to mental stimulation and clarity. Obviously, it is logical for parents to allow their children to consume caffeine, including coffee, in the morning for their well-being.

The author of Passage 1 would most likely criticize the author of Passage 2 for

A	relying heavily on statistics about the number of young people consuming caffeine
B	overlooking the possible negative effects of caffeine on young people
C	asserting that getting enough sleep is unimportant
D	exaggerating the physical health benefits of antioxidants

NOTES:

_____

_____

_____

This time, the question wants to know how the author of Passage 1 would **criticize** the author of Passage 2. Based on our **summaries**, Passage 1 is opposed to caffeine, whereas Passage 2 is in favor of caffeine. Let's use that difference to eliminate some answers:

Choice A is incorrect because the author of Passage 2 specifically did *not* rely on statistics.

Choice C is incorrect because the author of Passage 2 does not address the amount of sleep young people should be getting at all.

Choice D is incorrect because the author of Passage 1 does not express an opinion about *antioxidants*.

Choice B is correct because the author of Passage 1 is explicitly concerned with the *effects of caffeine on young people* and would find Passage 2's support for them consuming caffeine to be problematic.

NOTES:

Dual Passage, Practice Set Two

Passage

Passage 1

As secondary education options become more diverse, liberal arts colleges are gaining popularity. The size of liberal arts colleges usually allow the student population to be well acquainted with one another. Smaller class sizes also mean professors often have more one-on-one time with students. However, the cost of attendance may not be worth it, depending on what kind of lifestyle students expect to have in the future. Another option might be taking liberal arts classes at a state university rather than attending a private liberal arts school. This way, students can still receive a well-rounded education, while avoiding many years paying off student loans.

Passage 2

Many students today are choosing to go to a state university because of the greater number of opportunities available. Despite their "small classroom" advantages, private liberal arts schools can miss out on important government funding, so their facilities and resources can be lacking. Students may pay a higher tuition cost, spend more in student fees, and encounter higher prices in the cafeteria or recreation center. Ensuring job security after graduation is also crucial, and students are increasingly opting for majors that are perceived to lead more directly to jobs. A liberal arts college experience can be rewarding, but for many high school graduates, the high cost of tuition is not worth it.

Question 3 of 4

The author of Passage 1 would most likely criticize the author of Passage 2 for

Answers

A	exaggerating the number of students seeking core majors
B	disregarding the benefits of smaller class sizes
C	ignoring liberal arts classes available at state universities
D	underestimating the added costs of liberal arts schools

Question 4 of 4

Both authors would probably agree that, for some students, going to a liberal arts college is

Answers

A	essential
B	unaffordable
C	practical
D	unfulfilling

SECTION TWO, ELAR:
SENTENCE CORRECTION

SENTENCE CORRECTION, PRACTICE SET ONE

Question 1 of 6
To enter into the tournament, the student or <u>teacher have to</u> pay $10, and all of the proceeds go to help children with cancer.

	Answers
A	teacher have to
B	teacher has to
C	teacher must have to
D	teacher had to

Question 2 of 6
<u>With the advancement of identity theft, and some unsuspecting customers being</u> in very real danger.

	Answers
A	With the advancement of identity theft, and some unsuspecting customers being
B	With the advancement of identity theft, some unsuspecting customers are
C	With identity theft being how it is, some unsuspecting customers being
D	Identity theft being how it is, thus some unsuspecting customers being

Question 3 of 6
He can grow his own food, and he knows which kinds of wild berries and plants <u>are</u> safe to eat.

	Answers
A	are
B	is
C	being
D	that is

THE SENTENCE CORRECTION BASIC STRATEGY

Sentence Correction questions will provide a sentence with part (or all) of it underlined, along with four choices. The first choice **always** matches the original sentence, which means that sometimes the original sentence is grammatically correct.

THE BASIC STRATEGY

1. **Read the Sentence**
   This seems obvious, but you should start by reading the sentence to get your bearings.

2. **If It Sounds Wrong, Cross off Choice A and Any Choices That Repeat the Problem**
   If you can tell the original is wrong, that is enough to cross off choice A (choice A always repeats the original sentence). If you can **name the error**, that's even better.

   However, if you don't know if there is something wrong with the sentence, don't cross anything off just yet. Remember—if you don't see a problem, it might not have one!

3. **Compare the Rest of the Choices**
   The differences between the remaining choices should clue you in to what you need to do. For example, if the choices are only different because of the verb, the topic is probably verb tense or subject-verb agreement. If the remaining choices are all one-word transitions, you should be thinking about transitions.

4. **Use the Process of Elimination**
   Eliminate any choices that are grammatically incorrect.

   If you have multiple choices left over, pick the choice that has the **clearest** meaning to you.

NOTES:

_____

_____

_____

_____

_____

_____

Let's review the basic strategy by looking at the first question from the exercise:

Question 1 of 6
To enter into the tournament, the student or <u>teacher have to</u> pay $10, and all of the proceeds go to help children with cancer.

Answers		
A	teacher have to
B	teacher has to
C	teacher must have to
D	teacher had to

You can now see that this is an example of a **Sentence Correction** question type, and you should use the basic strategy covered on the previous page.

Hopefully you noticed that *the student or teacher have to pay* "sounded wrong" even if you aren't sure of what is causing the problem. We can now **eliminate choice A**. We should **also** eliminate choice C, since it repeats the problem (*have*).

Now, we need to decide between choices B and D. Even if you are stuck at this point, you've put yourself in a good position to make a solid guess. That said, since the rest of the sentence is in **present tense**, we should choose choice B.

NOTES:

_____

_____

_____

_____

_____

_____

_____

Now try this strategy out on your own with the following question:

Many people think it to be a myth or a hoax, some truly believe they have seen it.

A	Many people
B	Although many people
C	Groups
D	Research shows we

NOTES:

_____

_____

_____

_____

_____

_____

_____

_____

_____

_____

_____

_____

Ideally, you recognized that the original sentence has a problem: the sentence has a comma separating two independent clauses (*many people think it to be a myth or a hoax* and *some truly believe they have seen it*).

This is called a **comma splice** and, in this case, the best way to fix it is to use a **conjunction.** Remember that terminology isn't important on the TSIA2 ELAR test, but it can be helpful to know the names for grammatical issues. Either way, we should eliminate choices A, C, and D, since they repeat the problem.

That is enough to help us pick choice B, but it is helpful to see how choice B fixed the problem. Note that it used the conjunction *although* to connect these two sentences. That is a really common way to fix the comma splice error.

NOTES:

_____

_____

_____

_____

_____

_____

_____

_____

_____

_____

_____

_____

WHAT SOUNDS WRONG
IS WRONG

The good news about grammar is that you can usually recognize obviously bad grammar right away. We've already seen this in action during the basic strategy, but let's review the concept. Look at question two from the earlier exercise.

Question 2 of 6		
With the advancement of identity theft, and some unsuspecting customers being in very real danger.		

Answers		
A	With the advancement of identity theft, and some unsuspecting customers being
B	With the advancement of identity theft, some unsuspecting customers are
C	With identity theft being how it is, some unsuspecting customers being
D	Identity theft being how it is, thus some unsuspecting customers being

The big thing to know about "sounding it out" is that it works best as an **elimination** technique. In other words, it is easier to "hear" what is **incorrect**. Sometimes bad grammar can actually sound good, but good grammar almost **never** sounds bad.

With question two, it is easy to see right away that the sentence somehow sounds incomplete. Trust your gut and eliminate choice A and any other choice that sounds incomplete. In this case choices C and D are also "incomplete" sounding.

Just like that, you are left with the correct answer of choice B. If you want to **check twice**, you can also sound out choice B and ensure that it at least "sounds" good. In this case, it sounds just fine, so we are comfortable picking choice B as our answer.

NOTES:

_____

_____

This page is intentionally left blank.

Now give the Sounds Wrong strategy a try with the following question:

The habit of staying up all night to study is believed to be one of the best ways to prepare for a test; <u>frankly</u>, studies show stopping early to get a good night's sleep will improve your performance.

A	frankly
B	thus
C	in reality
D	furthermore

NOTES:

_____

_____

_____

_____

_____

_____

_____

_____

_____

_____

This time, you are looking at a transition. (Notice that every answer choice contains a transition word.) It can be a little tougher "sounding" this one out, but if you mentally read the entire sentence with each transition, you should be able to tell that something doesn't really make sense.

Try plugging each transition back in and sounding them out, one by one. (Remember, you have the time to do this.)

As it turns out, choices B and D sound a little off. The second part of the sentence is contradicting the first part, so *thus* and *furthermore* aren't the right fit. That leaves us with choices A and C.

At this point, if you aren't sure how to choose between the final two options, you can either **go with your gut** or pick the option that makes the **most sense** to you.

In this case, choice C is correct, since it correctly contrasts the first half and second half of the sentence.

NOTES:

_____

_____

_____

_____

_____

_____

_____

_____

_____

_____

KEEP IT CONSISTENT

A lot of grammar questions boil down to the issue of **consistency**. This can be anything from keeping verbs in the same tense to ensuring the transitions in a sentence make the best logical sense. In any case, if you aren't sure how to solve a grammar question, consider how each answer choice fits with the rest of the sentence. Here are a few points to watch for consistency:

- Subject-verb agreement
- Verb tense
- Pronoun agreement
- Sentence structure

Take a look at question three.

Question 3 of 6
He can grow his own food, and he knows which kinds of wild berries and plants <u>are</u> safe to eat.

Answers	
A	are
B	is
C	being
D	that is

The first thing you should notice is that the underlined portion here is a verb, specifically the verb *are*. Since *are* is a plural verb, meaning it is used with a plural subject, we can quickly check the **consistency**. In other words, *is there a plural subject*?

The subject in this case is *kinds of wild berries and plants*, which refers to more than one thing, so it is plural. That means we don't want a *singular* verb such as *is*, which eliminates choices B and D.

If you aren't sure about choice C, you can also use the Sounds Wrong strategy by plugging it back into the sentence and seeing how it works:

> He can grow his own food, and he knows which kinds of wild berries and plants **being** safe to eat.

It's a lot easier to either **see** or **hear** the problem when we put the answer choices back into the sentence. In this case, it lets us eliminate choice C and confirm that choice A is the correct answer.

In Sentence Correction questions, choice A is always the same as the original sentence, but don't let this discourage you from picking it! The option to make no changes to the sentence is the correct answer **just as often** as any other choice.

A NOTE ABOUT CHOICE A

Instead of thinking of it as "change" versus "no change," you should compare all four choices to see what is best. The keys to keep in mind are as follows:

- Choice A is correct just as often as any other choice, so don't be afraid to pick it!
- Don't focus on making changes and instead compare the choices against each other.
- If you spot something wrong right away, go ahead and eliminate choice A and continue on.

NOTES:

_____

_____

_____

_____

_____

_____

_____

_____

_____

_____

_____

_____

Look for consistency in the following question:

> Almost every student participates and <u>are</u> really competitive.

A	are
B	being
C	is
D	its

NOTES:

_____

_____

_____

_____

_____

_____

_____

_____

_____

_____

_____

One of the key areas in consistency is **subject-verb agreement**. In this case, each answer choice contains a verb, so you might be tempted to find the subject. However, the subject in this question is hard to find. Is it *student* or is it *every student*, and does that even matter? If you ever get in this position, try to match the verb to the **other verbs** in the sentence.

In this case, the other verb in the sentence is *participates*. This is an example of a **singular** verb (remember that regular, singular, present tense verbs end with *s* or *es*). With that in mind, the only available option that is also a singular verb is *is*, which makes choice C the correct answer.

NOTES:

_____

_____

_____

_____

_____

_____

_____

_____

_____

_____

_____

SENTENCE CORRECTION, PRACTICE SET TWO

Question 4 of 6
Almost every applicant passes and <u>are</u> very successful.

Answers	
A	are
B	is
C	its
D	being

Question 5 of 6
Seahorses eat <u>with the use of</u> their snouts to suck up plankton or crustaceans, and they use their tails to hook onto seagrass or coral.

Answers	
A	with the use of
B	in using
C	by using
D	for use of

Question 6 of 6
In the 1930s, a picture was taken of "Nessie," and people debate <u>their</u> authenticity to this day.

Answers	
A	their
B	its
C	it's
D	its'

SECTION TWO, ELAR:
PASSAGE CORRECTION

Passage Correction, Practice Set One

Passage

(1) Technology could one day be driving your car. (2) It is more than just the power behind texting or video games. (3) According to the latest research, technology may soon replace human drivers in the form of self-driving cars.

(4) Up until recently, autopilots were common on planes or in agricultural harvesting, but development of the self-driving car never saw significant progress. (5) One reason why self-driving cars have yet to take off as a modern commuting option is the fact that they must navigate intricate and complex roadways. (6) In contrast, the air, sea, and even the surface of Mars are far simpler, with no traffic lights or stray children to run into the path. (7) For years, autonomous submarines have roamed wide-open waters, and driverless trains have followed limited, straightforward tracks.

(8) A second reason for the delay in the development of self-driving cars is that they require specialized, up-to-date maps. (9) Modern technology is teeming with online maps and GPS programs. (10) However, for self-driving cars to be successful, GPS isn't sufficient; a reliable backup system is necessary. (11) "We are currently developing artificial intelligence that allows an automated car to navigate new roads without [the use of] 3D maps, using a series of sensors that observe road conditions," Leslie Sanchez, chief engineer at Plymouth Labs, said.

(12) New car models include features that take over driving if the car swerves out of its lane or if vehicles in front of it stop suddenly. (13) These are examples of self-driving technology. (14) They say self-driving cars will lower the frequency of accidents on the road and reduce traffic.

Question 1 of 6

In context, which of the following sentences would best be inserted between sentences 9 and 10?

Answers

A	Recent developments indicate that driverless cars may also one day replace ambulance drivers responding to emergencies.
B	Developing backup technology will likely take another decade.
C	Garmin Ltd., for example, provides GPS and mapping for a variety of users.
D	Many think self-driving cars could one day replace taxis and buses.

Question 2 of 6

In context, which of the following is the best way to revise and combine sentences 1 and 2 (reproduced below)?

Technology could one day be driving your car. It is more than just the power behind texting or video games.

	Answers
A	Technology could one day be driving your car, it is more than just the power behind texting or video games.
B	Technology could one day be driving your car because it is more than just the power behind texting or video games.
C	Technology is more than just the power behind texting or video games; it could one day be driving your car.
D	Technology could one day be driving your car, so it is more than just the power behind texting or video games.

Question 3 of 6

In context, where would the following sentence best be placed?

There are several explanations for this.

	Answers
A	After sentence 1
B	After sentence 4
C	After sentence 6
D	After sentence 9

The Passage Correction Basic Strategy

Passage Correction questions provide an entire passage that is around 250 words long, typically made up of three or more paragraphs. The passage is paired with a group of questions, usually three.

Take a look back at the practice set. Note that all three questions belong to the same passage.

In order to tackle **Passage Correction** questions, you'll need a good strategy.

The Basic Strategy

1. **Read the Passage**
   You might be tempted to start with the questions, but a lot of Passage Correction questions focus on the **big picture**, so it's important to work through the passage first.

2. **Determine the Question Type**
   There are two types of questions.
   - **Grammar:** These questions are just like Sentence Correction questions, and they will ask about the grammar of a specific part of the passage.
   - **Composition:** These questions will ask you to alter the passage composition by deleting unnecessary information, combining sentences, and other editing tasks.

3. **Use the Right Strategy**
   If the question is asking about the **grammar**, use the strategies you have already learned in the earlier parts of this chapter.

   If the question is focused on the **composition**, use the strategies covered later in this section.

4. **Use the Process of Elimination**
   Eliminate any choices that you **know** don't work. Then compare what is left and pick the option that you think is the best remaining choice.

NOTES:

_____

_____

_____

_____

Give it a try on the first question.

First, read the passage. This passage is about technology that could enable driverless cars and some of the limitations and developments related to that technology.

Now, look at the question:

Question 1 of 6
In context, which of the following sentences would best be inserted between sentences 9 and 10?

	Answers
A	Recent developments indicate that driverless cars may also one day replace ambulance drivers responding to emergencies.
B	Developing backup technology will likely take another decade.
C	Garmin Ltd., for example, provides GPS and mapping for a variety of users.
D	Many think self-driving cars could one day replace taxis and buses.

This question specifically asks what should be inserted between sentences 9 and 10. The best way to tackle this is to consider the **content** of both sentences. Then, fit the most **relevant** sentence in the middle:

> **Sentence 9:** *Modern technology is teeming with online maps and GPS programs.*

Sentence 9 focuses on **current modern technology** for **online maps** and **GPS**.

> **Sentence 10:** *However, for self-driving cars to be successful, GPS isn't sufficient; a reliable backup system is necessary.*

Sentence 10 uses the word *however* to indicate a shift from **GPS** to the need for a **backup system**.

The best sentence to insert between these two sentences will focus on **GPS** and other modern **mapping technology**.

Choice B comes **too early** in the paragraph, since *backup* technology doesn't get introduced until sentence 10. Choice D doesn't focus on GPS or mapping, so we can eliminate it. Choice A is incorrect because it focuses on *driverless cars* and *ambulance drivers*, which doesn't connect to the following sentence.

That leaves choice C, which gives a modern example of GPS and mapping technology.

This page is intentionally left blank.

Try it out on another example, using the passage from the exercise:

In context, which is the best revision to sentence 14 (reproduced below)? *They say self-driving cars will lower the frequency of accidents on the road and reduce traffic.*	

A	Replace "They say" with "Developers argue".
B	Replace "will lower" with "will reduce".
C	Delete "and reduce traffic".
D	Insert "their" before "accidents".

NOTES:

_____

_____

_____

_____

_____

_____

_____

_____

_____

_____

_____

This time, the question wants us to fix the grammar in the sentence. You can eliminate choices B and D because they make unnecessary changes. Choice C can also be ruled out because it takes away from the meaning of the sentence.

Choice A is the best revision because it **clarifies** the pronoun *they* by explicitly stating who is making the argument about self-driving cars.

NOTES:

_____

_____

_____

_____

_____

_____

_____

_____

_____

_____

_____

COMBINING SENTENCES

Passage Correction questions will sometimes ask you to **combine** two of the sentences in the essay. There are a number of things to keep in mind in this situation:

- The combined sentence needs to be **complete.**
- The combined sentence cannot be a **comma splice** or a **run-on sentence.**
- The connection between the sentences needs to make sense.
- Get the Main Idea and Sounds Wrong are **really useful** strategies here.

Take a look at the second question on the exercise:

Question 2 of 6
In context, which of the following is the best way to revise and combine sentences 1 and 2 (reproduced below)? *Technology could one day be driving your car. It is more than just the power behind texting or video games.*

	Answers
A	Technology could one day be driving your car, it is more than just the power behind texting or video games.
B	Technology could one day be driving your car because it is more than just the power behind texting or video games.
C	Technology is more than just the power behind texting or video games; it could one day be driving your car.
D	Technology could one day be driving your car, so it is more than just the power behind texting or video games.

Choice A is a **comma splice**, two sentences conjoined by only a comma, so it can be eliminated.

Technology being more than *just the power behind texting or video games* is not exactly a reason that technology could one day be driving cars, so the transition word *because* in choice B does not make sense.

Choice D is grammatically correct, but it is not the best fit, because a major point in the essay is technology eventually driving cars, not simply that technology is more than the power behind texting and video games.

Choice C connects the two sentences with a **semicolon**, which is an acceptable way to connect two related sentences, so it is the correct answer. Furthermore, this sentence correctly puts the focus on the idea that technology *could one day be driving your car*, which is the topic of the essay.

This page is intentionally left blank.

Try these tips on your own with the following question:

What is the best way to combine sentences 12 and 13 at the underlined part (reproduced below)?

New car models include features that take over driving if the car swerves out of its lane or if vehicles in front of it stop suddenly. These are examples of self-driving technology.

A	stop suddenly, this is an example
B	stop suddenly these features are examples
C	stop suddenly, which are examples
D	stop suddenly, for instance, these are examples

NOTES:

_____

_____

_____

_____

_____

_____

_____

_____

_____

_____

In this example, only a part of each sentence is underlined. However, the strategy is still the same.

Choices A, B, and D are either **comma splices** or **run-on sentences**, a combination of two sentences without proper connectors or punctuation.

Choice C correctly connects the two sentences with *which*.

NOTES:

_____

_____

_____

_____

_____

_____

_____

_____

_____

_____

_____

_____

SEQUENCING

One of the unique types of questions you'll see on the test will ask you to insert a new sentence somewhere into the essay. These can be tricky, so they deserve their own strategy:

1. **Read the New Sentence**
   Determine the topic of the sentence and look for any **clues** on where to place it.

2. **Try Out Each Choice**
   Put the new sentence in the location in each answer choice and see how it fits. Look at the topic of the sentences **before** and **after** the new sentence and look for any connections.

3. **Use the Process of Elimination**
   Eliminate any choices that are:

   - **too early** in the essay.

   - **out of order** with the rest of the sentences.

   - **not connected** to the surrounding sentences.

NOTES:

_____

_____

_____

_____

_____

_____

_____

_____

_____

Consider the third question in the exercise:

Question 3 of 6
In context, where would the following sentence best be placed?
There are several explanations for this.

	Answers
A	After sentence 1
B	After sentence 4
C	After sentence 6
D	After sentence 9

The new sentence sets up the essay to list several reasons for something. Insert the sentence at each point and see how it works. We'll look at the three **incorrect** options first:

> **Choice A:** (1) Technology could one day be driving your car. **There are several explanations for this.** (2) It is more than just the power behind texting or video games.

The concept of *explanations* doesn't make logical sense at this point in the essay.

> **Choice B:** (6) In contrast, the air, sea, and even the surface of Mars are far simpler with no traffic lights or stray children to run into the path. **There are several explanations for this.** (7) For years, autonomous submarines have roamed wide-open waters and driverless trains have followed limited, straightforward tracks.

Because the explanations were given back in sentence 5, this choice is **out of order**.

> **Choice D:** (9) Modern technology is teeming with online maps and GPS programs. **There are several explanations for this.** (10) However, for self-driving cars to be successful, GPS isn't sufficient; a reliable backup system is necessary.

The use of the word *however* in sentence 10 is a huge sign that we don't want to insert our new sentence here. The insertion **breaks up the connection** of the ideas between sentences 9 and 10.

Finally, look at the correct answer:

> **Choice C:** (4) Up until recently, autopilots were common on planes or in agricultural harvesting, but development of the self-driving car never saw significant progress. **There are several explanations for this.** (5) One reason why self-driving cars have avoided advancement is the fact that they must navigate intricate and complex roadways.

Notice how well the new sentence fits into this part of the essay. The idea of *explanations* **connects** the problem discussed in sentence 4 to the *reason* that follows in sentence 5.

Give it a try on the following question, using the same passage:

Where in the second paragraph should the following sentence best be inserted? *This has allowed for the development of some self-driving vehicles.*	

A	Immediately after sentence 4
B	Immediately after sentence 5
C	Immediately after sentence 6
D	Immediately after sentence 7

NOTES:

_____

_____

_____

_____

_____

_____

_____

_____

_____

_____

This time, you need to look at the second paragraph, but the strategy is the same. This sentence adds information about the *self-driving vehicles*.

The most logical location is to put this right before the *autonomous submarines*, a type of *self-driving vehicle*, in sentence 7, making choice C the best answer.

NOTES:

_____

_____

_____

_____

_____

_____

_____

_____

_____

_____

_____

_____

_____

Passage Correction, Practice Set Two

Passage

(1) Why do some people enjoy being scared? (2) You might be someone who happily pays money for scary movies, haunted houses, or terrifying thrill rides. (3) There's actually a scientific explanation behind this affinity. (4) Social psychologist Dr. Clark McCauley of Bryn Mawr College explains it like this: "The fictional nature of horror films affords viewers a sense of control by placing psychological distance between them and the violent acts they have witnessed." (5) Dr. McCauley received his PhD from the University of Pennsylvania.

(6) Research has shown that stressed or anxious viewers actually feel better after watching horror movies. (7) They ultimately help by allowing their brains to artificially focus on survival instead of the issues in their lives that were previously causing worry or fear. (8) When you're scared, your prefrontal cortex, responsible for planning and decision-making, becomes overshadowed by the limbic system, which controls arousal and stimulation. (9) Coming down from this adrenaline rush gives anxious viewers a sense of calm when a movie finishes, so it is not uncommon for sufferers to seek thrills and scares for therapeutic purposes.

Question 4 of 6

What is the best way to combine sentences 6 and 7 at the underlined part (reproduced below)?

Research has shown that stressed or anxious viewers actually feel better after watching <u>horror movies. They ultimately help</u> by allowing their brains to artificially focus on survival instead of the issues in their lives that were previously causing worry or fear.

Answers

A	horror movies, these ultimately help
B	horror movies ultimately these movies help
C	horror movies, which ultimately help
D	horror movies; then, they ultimately help

Question 5 of 6

Which of the following sentences is irrelevant information that can be deleted from the passage?

Answers

A	Sentence 1
B	Sentence 3
C	Sentence 5
D	Sentence 8

Question 6 of 6
Where in the second paragraph should the following sentence be inserted?
These fears are temporarily calmed by the body.

Answers	
A	Immediately after sentence 6
B	Immediately after sentence 7
C	Immediately after sentence 8
D	Immediately after sentence 9

Section Two, ELAR:
Writing the Essay

An Introduction to the TSIA2 Essay

The TSIA2 Essay contains exactly one prompt that requires you to write between 300 and 600 words. Your essay is scored on a different scale than the other tests, from 1 to 8, and it is considered in conjunction with your score from the multiple-choice section of the ELAR test.

There are two ways to get the score you need:

- Score a **945 or higher** on the multiple-choice section and score a **5 or higher** on the essay.
- Score a **5 or 6** on the Diagnostic Test and a **5 or higher** on the essay.

The essay is scored according to your performance in the following areas:

- **Purpose and Focus:** This refers to staying on topic as you write and having a clear main idea.
- **Organization and Structure:** This area is concerned with keeping your ideas organized, typically through paragraphs.
- **Development and Support:** This is all about elaboration and using evidence to back up your main idea.
- **Sentence Variety and Style:** This area focuses on your use of sentence structure and vocabulary.
- **Mechanical Conventions:** This is specifically about your correct use of grammar and punctuation.
- **Critical Thinking:** The last area reviews the logic of your ideas.

The key to doing well is to maximize each of these categories to the best of your ability with the **goal of scoring a 5**.

NOTES:

_____

_____

_____

_____

_____

_____

Let's take a look at what it takes to score a 5.

SCORING A 5

An essay in this category demonstrates **adequate mastery** of on-demand essay writing. A typical essay:

- Develops a **viable point of view** on the issue
- May stray from the audience and purpose but **is able to refocus**
- Demonstrates **competent critical thinking**, using adequate examples, reason, and other evidence to support its position
- Is generally organized and focused but could lack coherence and logical progression of ideas
- Exhibits adequate but inconsistent control of language
- Contains some minor errors in sentence structure, grammar, spelling, and punctuation

---

This rubric is adapted from accuplacer.collegeboard.org/accuplacer/pdf/tsia-interpreting-your-score-brochure.pdf.

There are a few key points to take away from the scoring guidelines:

- Your **opinion** matters—make sure you clearly state it.
- Use **examples** and **explain** them thoroughly.
- Organize your essay using **paragraphs** and **topic sentences**.
- Double-check your **grammar** and **spelling!**

NOTES:

_____

_____

_____

_____

THE PROMPT

The prompt on the TSIA2 has a unique format that you'll need to consider before you write your essay. Consider the following example:

PASSAGE

An athlete, during her final workout of the week, was unable to complete the last drill. She said, "I can't do it, I'm too tired." And the coach said, "Try anyway. If you feel like you can't, you can still choose to push through it. If you fear failure, you can still give it your all." From this experience, the athlete learned that with any goal in life that feels impossible, there is always the determination to try anyway.

Adapted from Marzi Baracas, "Net Work"

ASSIGNMENT

Can any fatigue or weakness be overcome by willpower?

Each prompt contains two parts: the **Passage** and the **Assignment**.

- The **passage** is there for context—you should **not** write about the passage in your essay.
- The **assignment** is the part that you care about. You **must** develop and defend an opinion in response to the assignment.

NOTES:

_____

_____

_____

_____

_____

_____

_____

HOW TO WRITE THE ESSAY

The key to writing an essay that addresses the **prompt** and scores as many points as possible is to have a clear plan. Don't just start writing as soon as you read the prompt!

THE ESSAY GAME PLAN

1. **Decide Your Opinion**
    This is also known as a **thesis**. You're going to need it when you start writing.

    If you don't really have an opinion, you need to **make one up**. The TSIA2 isn't scoring your *real* opinion on a topic; it is only looking at how well you defend *an* opinion.

2. **Choose Your Examples**
    You will need **exactly two** solid examples to support your opinion. Pull your examples from the following:

    - **Fiction**: This can be from books, television, movies, or even graphic novels.
    - **History**: Anything from ancient history to modern history and from any culture is acceptable.
    - **Current Events**: Write on recent happenings in the news, but be careful not to be too controversial.

    Notice that none of the topics include **personal experience**. While this is technically accepted, it is usually not easy to pull off correctly. Use personal experiences only if you have no other ideas.

3. **Write the Introduction**
    It's time to write! Aim for your introduction to be about 3−4 sentences long. Your intro should **start** with a general statement and **end** with your opinion and a preview of your examples.

    Be direct when you state your opinion. Don't use the phrase *in my opinion*.

4. **Write Two Body Paragraphs**
    You will write a body paragraph based on each of your **examples**. Each paragraph should **start** with a topic sentence describing your example and how it relates. The **rest of the paragraph** should elaborate on the example and support your overall point.

    Aim for 4−5 sentences in total per paragraph.

5. **Write the Conclusion**
    Every essay **requires** a conclusion. If you don't wrap up your ideas in a **separate concluding paragraph**, you will automatically lose points.

    Start your conclusion with a restatement of your opinion. Add another sentence or two that recaps your examples, then **close** with a general statement about the essay topic.

6. **Review**
    This is the least exciting step, but it is important. You should review your essay, looking for any **grammar** or **spelling** errors before submitting. You only need to spend 5 minutes on this step, but you could save your essay an entire point if you catch and fix your errors.

    When you review, it is also worth considering the following:

    - Is your **opinion** very clear?
    - Did you **support** your opinion with good examples?
    - Did you **elaborate** on your examples enough?
    - Does everything make **sense?**
    - Did you use any **vocabulary** incorrectly?

Let's try it out on the prompt we saw earlier:

PASSAGE

An athlete, during her final workout of the week, was unable to complete the last drill. She said, "I can't do it, I'm too tired." And the coach said, "Try anyway. If you feel like you can't, you can still choose to push through it. If you fear failure, you can still give it your all." From this experience, the athlete learned that with any goal in life that feels impossible, there is always the determination to try anyway.

Adapted from Marzi Baracas, "Net Work"

ASSIGNMENT

Can any fatigue or weakness be overcome by willpower?

Opinion: _____

_____

_____

_____

Example One: _____

_____

_____

_____

Example Two: _____

_____

_____

_____

Put it all together and write an **introductory paragraph**:

Next, write just the first **example paragraph**:

_____

_____

_____

_____

_____

_____

_____

_____

_____

_____

_____

_____

_____

_____

_____

_____

_____

_____

_____

_____

_____

_____

_____

_____

_____

Now, write just the second **example paragraph**:

Finally, wrap it all up with your **conclusion paragraph:**

_____

_____

_____

_____

_____

_____

_____

_____

_____

_____

_____

_____

_____

_____

_____

_____

_____

_____

_____

_____

_____

_____

_____

_____

_____

WRITE LIKE A PRO

There are a few things you can do to improve your essay, beyond forming an opinion and supporting it with good examples.

- Use the **active voice** and avoid weak statements such as *in my opinion* or *I think*. Be confident and state your points directly.

- Write a good **hook** to catch the reader right at the start of your essay.
  - For example, you could use a quotation (it's okay if it isn't exact), ask the reader a rhetorical question, or even make a joke.

- Use **transitions** at the start of your two example paragraphs. Even simple ones such as *first of all* or *moreover* go a long way.

- Use **descriptive language** to elaborate even further on your examples. If you can paint a mental picture, it will sell your point more effectively.

- Address a **counterargument** in your example paragraphs to improve the argumentation in your essay.

None of these are necessary to hit a 5 on your essay, but they can help you lock in your score more easily.

NOTES:

_____

_____

_____

_____

_____

_____

_____

_____

_____

_____

TSIA2 ESSAY PRACTICE

Try it out with an essay of your own using the following prompt:

PASSAGE

"I learned that courage was not the absence of fear, but the triumph over it. The brave man is not he who does not feel afraid, but he who conquers that fear." —Nelson Mandela

ASSIGNMENT

Are we in control of our fears? Explain why or why not.

SAMPLE ESSAY RESPONSE

While fear serves as a healthy instinct to keep us safe, these days modern medicine, governments, and technology allow us to live more safely and comfortably than ever before. The fear that remains in our lives is often not an indicator of a true threat or danger. Instead, it comes from our own misgivings about ourselves and what we can accomplish. This can be seen in Meg Murray from *A Wrinkle in Time*, who overcomes self-doubt to save her family, and in real-life pilot Captain Sullenberger, who quieted his fears in order to successfully carry out an emergency landing of a damaged plane. Modern fear comes from within and can be overcome, leading to accomplishment and fulfillment.

The main character of *A Wrinkle in Time*, Meg Murray, was afraid to join her brother in search for their lost father. Through each leg of the journey, she had to be pushed along by others or have her hand held, literally. The disappearance of her father felt like abandonment and had left Meg unmotivated and full of self-doubt for several years. This inner struggle caused her to fear the journey necessary to save her family. Toward the end of the book, when she risked also losing her brother, Meg realized that her fear had not been about the possibility of physical harm during the journey but about her own lack of self-confidence and independence. When she set aside this fear, she realized she was, in fact, capable of facing challenges alone, and she was able to save both her father and brother. Once Meg understood she had nothing to be afraid of and that her own mind had been holding her back, she was able to take control of her fear and accomplish her goal, reuniting her family.

The famous pilot Chesley Sullenberger, or Sully, successfully landed a commercial airplane on the Hudson River despite the emotions he felt during such a terrifying situation. Shortly after takeoff, the flight incurred damage to both engines, and Sullenberger was forced to execute an emergency landing. Unable to reach an airport, he piloted the plane toward the Hudson River, where he would successfully complete a water landing. Sullenberger describes the moments before the landing as the most sickening and terrifying experience of his life. He doubted his ability to land the plane and save the lives on board. However, when Sullenberger resolved to trust his training and experience, he was able to take meaningful action. Because he chose to control his fear and not to listen to the doubts in his mind, his true ability shined through. He successfully landed the plane and saved all the lives on board.

The fear many people experience today is in their heads and can be controlled. This is evident in both literature and real life, as seen in the stories of Meg Murray and Chesley Sullenberger. Moreover, all of us can learn from these experiences, silence the fears that limit us, and go on to conquer our goals.

ELAR WRAP-UP

Remember the following key points when you tackle the ELAR test on the TSIA2:

- Use the **basic strategy** for each question type:
  - **Short Passage**
  - **Long Passage**
  - **Dual Passage**
  - **Sentence Correction**
  - **Passage Correction**
- Apply the different strategies covered in this chapter:
  - Get the Main Idea
  - Drawing Conclusions
  - Finding Meaning
  - Point of View
  - Agree to Disagree
  - Comparing and Contrasting
  - Sounds Wrong Is Wrong
  - Keep It Consistent

For further practice, visit accuplacerpractice.collegeboard.org.

NOTES:

_____

_____

_____

_____

_____

_____

_____

ELAR ANSWER EXPLANATIONS

SHORT PASSAGE, PRACTICE SET ONE

1. **The correct answer is C.** The paragraph describes international cleanup days where volunteers clean up waste in their country. The movement is described as aiming to *combat the global solid waste problem*. This best aligns with the goal described in choice C. Choice A is incorrect because, while the organization does value nature, its goal with the cleanup days was not to have people spend more time in nature. Choice B is incorrect because it refers broadly to volunteering, rather than the more specific act of helping the environment. Choice D is incorrect because, though many countries are involved, their shared goal is preserving the planet, not interacting with each other. Only choice C matches the organization's purpose as described in the paragraph.

2. **The correct answer is D.** The passage explains the surprising fact that stomachs can blush just as much as the face. Choice A is incorrect this topic is too narrow and only describes one part of the passage. Choice B is incorrect because it is an explanatory detail included in the passage, not the main idea. Choice C is incorrect because it exaggerates the facts stated in passage. Choice D is correct because it matches the focus of the passage.

3. **The correct answer is B.** This paragraph describes the pleasing, rich aroma of the olive oil and the narrator's memories of her *nonna* using it in various dishes. Choices A and C contradict the positive feelings described, while choice D is unsupported by the passage. Choice B is correct because the narrator associates the aroma of olive oil with warm memories.

SHORT PASSAGE, PRACTICE SET TWO

4. **The correct answer is C.** Choice A is incorrect because the passage indicates that the rising in pitch has occurred over the past 150 years, which implies that it began before the modern era. Choice B is incorrect because the passage does not indicate that the falsetto register caused tuning pitch to rise. Choice D is incorrect because the passage does not mention a new invention. Choice C is correct because the passage indicates that the rising in pitch has occurred over the past 150 years.

5. **The correct answer is B.** The passage defines a word and gives the history behind its meaning. Choice A is incorrect because it is too broad, leaving out *why* the passage is telling this tale. Choice C is incorrect because the story cautions against self-love, not love in general. Choice D is incorrect because while Narcissus struggles with unrequited love, it is not the main idea of the passage. Choice B correctly identifies the purpose of the passage, which details the history of a word.

6. **The correct answer is A.** The passage describes how a highly industrialized region primarily features classes on mechanical operations and how a tropical region—presumably a very warm climate—features classes on operating and maintaining air conditioners. This indicates that the BNVS curriculum is tailored to meet what would be most needed in the locale surrounding each campus. Choice B is incorrect because, though the schools do offer a wide array of class options, the purpose behind these options is to offer classes that would be the most useful to students in each region. Choice C is incorrect because there is nothing stated or implied in the passage about BNVS trying not to compete with other trade schools. Choice D is incorrect because government regulations are not mentioned in this passage. Choice A is correct because the second sentence states that BNVS offers *tailor-made courses that place graduates directly into employment in their geographical region.*

LONG PASSAGE, PRACTICE SET ONE

1. **The correct answer is D.** Choice A is incorrect because the passage does not discuss how *others can become philosophers as well*. Choice B is incorrect because the passage never indicates that Dennett could only ask questions that no one could answer. Choice C is incorrect because this is not the main point of the passage. Choice D is correct because the passage begins by examining Dennett's early years in school and concludes with Dennett becoming established in the academic world as a respected philosopher.

2. **The correct answer is C.** Choice A is incorrect because there is no indication that Dennett believed only his own opinions were valid. Choice B is incorrect because while the passage discusses Quine, there is no evidence that this phrase belonged to him. Choice D is incorrect because while the passage does indicate that Dennett wished to disprove Quine, it does not imply that they did not respect one another. Choice C is correct because the last paragraph states that Dennett had a path *he chose to follow* and that *he was the one calling the shots*, implying Dennett was forming his own theories.

3. **The correct answer is D.** The third paragraph describes Dennett's career in philosophy as choosing *to follow the path of questioning established truths*, giving him purpose and inspiring self-confidence. Philosophy is also described as being full of *daunting complexities*. This conveys that the field is challenging but fulfilling to Dennett. Choice A is incorrect because philosophy is not compared to science in the passage. Choice B is incorrect because it was Dennett's career, not a hobby, and he was very invested in it. Choice C is incorrect because there is no evidence Dennett thinks philosophy is useless. Choice D is supported by details in the third paragraph, so it is the correct answer.

LONG PASSAGE, PRACTICE SET TWO

4. **The correct answer is D.** This sentence describes the large infestation of fleas on Nibbie, and so the narrator is contrasting Nibbie's size with this volume of fleas. Choices A, B, and C are unsupported by the passage. Only choice D captures the contrast embedded in *sustain his population*, which implies his body was too small to be home to so many fleas.

5. **The correct answer is B.** The first paragraph describes Nibbie's abandonment by his original owners. Because the owners' actions are deliberate, choices A and C can be eliminated. Choice D is half right: Nibbie crawled under a car, but not because the author lost him. Choice B is correct because *meaning to lose him* conveys that Nibbie's original owners were attempting to abandon him.

6. **The correct answer is D.** Choice A is too extreme and is contradicted by the fact that Nibbie carried a hurt bird *without doing the least injury* to it. Choices B and C are unsupported by the passage. Right after the phrase *retrieving blood*, the narrator describes how Nibbie brought over an oriole without *doing the least injury to the bird*, suggesting that he may have characteristics of retrieving dogs, similar to his other behaviors related to potential breeds, mentioned earlier in the paragraph. Thus, choice D is the best answer.

DUAL PASSAGE, PRACTICE SET ONE

1. **The correct answer is D.** Choice A is incorrect because the author of Passage 2 does not refer to injuries. Choice B is incorrect because the author does not indicate she's unable to finish her homework in time. Choice C is incorrect because the author does not describe away games or how they disrupt her studies. Choice D is the correct answer because the author describes *mandatory study hall to keep our GPA up*, which indicates she spends many hours studying to maintain a high grade point average.

2. **The correct answer is B.** Passage 1 explains that student athletes have healthy habits in place, and Passage 2 describes grueling and exhausting workouts. This implies that both authors assume athletes are healthy as a result of their consistent physical exercise. Choice A is incorrect because only the author of Passage 2 would support *overwhelmed*; Passage 1 does not indicate student athletes might feel this way. Choice C is incorrect because the author of Passage 2 describes having friends and spending time with them. Choice D is incorrect because neither passage makes this claim. Choice B is the best answer because there is evidence in both passages to support it.

DUAL PASSAGE, PRACTICE SET TWO

3. **The correct answer is C.** The author of Passage 1 describes a compromise to the challenge of choosing between a private liberal arts or public state school: take liberal arts classes at a state school. The author of Passage 2 does not consider this middle ground, but rather takes a staunch stance against liberal arts altogether. Choice A is incorrect because the author of Passage 2 does not specify how many students are choosing core majors. Choice B is incorrect because the author of Passage 2 does acknowledge *"small classroom" advantages.* Choice D is incorrect because the author of Passage 2 acknowledges there can be extra costs when attending a liberal arts college. Only choice C accurately describes the details in Passage 2, making it the best answer.

4. **The correct answer is B.** The author of Passage 1 praises liberal arts schools, but admits many students suffer from the cost of attendance, spending *years paying off student loans.* The author of Passage 2 also states that at liberal arts schools, students pay a higher tuition, have more expenses, and might not have high-paying jobs after graduation. Choice A is incorrect because neither author describes attending a liberal arts college as *essential* for students. Choice C is incorrect because both authors cite the financial challenges of attending liberal arts schools, a factor that would not make them *practical.* Choice D is incorrect because both authors acknowledge the positive and fulfilling potential of a liberal arts education, so they would not describe it as *unfulfilling.* Only choice B correctly conveys a detail agreed upon by both authors, so it is the correct answer.

SENTENCE CORRECTION, PRACTICE SET ONE

1. **The correct answer is B.** The compound subject *student or teacher* is singular. The subject is describing the student *or* the teacher, that is, one or the other, but not both. Therefore *has*, the singular verb, is the correct verb. Choice A is incorrect because it uses the plural form *have.* Choice C is incorrect because *must* and *have to* together are redundant. Choice D is incorrect because it uses the past tense, which is not consistent with the present tense of the surrounding context.

2. **The correct answer is B.** The phrase *with the advancement of identity theft* is a prepositional phrase, so it should be joined to an independent clause with a comma only. The independent clause requires the verb *are* to be a complete sentence. Choice A is incorrect because it uses the participle *being*, creating a sentence fragment, and incorrectly joins a prepositional phrase with a comma and a conjunction. Choices C and D are incorrect because they also use the participle *being* instead of a verb.

3. **The correct answer is A.** The sentence correctly uses the plural verb *are* to agree with the plural subject *kinds.* Choices B and D are incorrect because they use the singular form *is.* Choice C is incorrect because *being* is a participle and therefore does not function as a verb, which is needed to complete the independent clause.

SENTENCE CORRECTION, PRACTICE SET TWO

4. **The correct answer is B.** The verb *is* is the correct singular verb to go with the singular subject, *applicant*. Choice A is incorrect because it leaves the verb in a plural form. Choice C does not contain a verb, so it is also incorrect. Choice D is incorrect because it uses the word *being*, which is a participle and not a verb.

5. **The correct answer is C.** The preposition *by* tells the reader that what comes next shows how the seahorses eat. *With* is somewhat awkward and does not communicate what the author is saying as clearly, so choice A is incorrect. Choice B is incorrect because saying the seahorses eat *in using* their snouts is not idiomatic. Choice D is incorrect because it confuses the intended meaning of the sentence.

6. **The correct answer is B.** The sentence is describing the quality of a single photo, so it should be written with the singular possessive *its* rather than the plural possessive *their*, making choice A incorrect. Choice C is incorrect because *it's* is a contraction for *it is* and is not the possessive form needed for this sentence. *Its'* is always incorrect, so choice D can be eliminated immediately.

PASSAGE CORRECTION, PRACTICE SET ONE

1. **The correct answer is C.** Sentence 9 asserts that digital mapping and GPS exist in abundance in today's society. Sentence 10 goes on to explain why this still may not be enough to power self-driving cars. The sentence that comes between these should be a continuation of sentence 9 or an introduction to sentence 10. Choice A is incorrect because it is unrelated to the passage. Choice B is incorrect because it continues the thought in sentence 10, so it should not precede this sentence. Choice D is incorrect because, while it is related to the topic of the passage, it is not related to the information in sentences 9 and 10. Choice C gives examples for the claim in sentence 9 and helps set up a strong contrast to the information that follows, making it the best answer.

2. **The correct answer is C.** Choice A is incorrect because two independent clauses cannot be separated by a comma alone. Choice B is incorrect because the transition *because* does not make sense in the context of the sentence. Choice D is incorrect because while it is grammatically correct, it misses the major point of the essay, which is that technology could be driving your car, so it is not the best fit. Only choice C combines the sentences in a logical manner and does not introduce any grammatical errors.

3. **The correct answer is B.** The passage lists two main reasons for why the technology needed for self-driving cars has progressed slowly. The idea is first introduced in sentence 4, followed by the first reason. Therefore, it makes the most sense to insert this sentence between sentences 4 and 5. Choice A is incorrect because it confuses the meaning of the paragraph. The technology of texting and video games is not a reason that *technology could one day be driving your car*. Choices C and D are incorrect because they are not claims followed by reasons, making this addition unnecessary and illogical. Only choice B correctly places the new sentence between a claim and the reasons that follow, so it is the correct answer.

PASSAGE CORRECTION, PRACTICE SET TWO

4. **The correct answer is C.** The antecedent of the pronoun *they* in sentence 7 is unclear and needs to be corrected. Choices A and B are incorrect because the changes create run-on sentences. Choice D is incorrect because it does not resolve the pronoun-antecedent ambiguity and introduces an unnecessary transition word. Only choice C removes the ambiguous pronoun and correctly links a dependent clause to the independent clause that precedes it.

5. **The correct answer is C.** The university where the psychologist obtained his degree is not relevant to the topic of the passage or the paragraph, which focuses on how artificially frightening circumstances can result in calmed anxiety. Choices A, B, and D are incorrect because they all include details that support the passage topic. Therefore, choice C is the best answer.

6. **The correct answer is B.** *These fears* implies that the fears have already been described, so the new sentence should come only after this description. Choice A is incorrect because fears have not been specifically introduced yet. Choice C is incorrect because it explains how fears are calmed by the body, so it should appear after, not before, the added sentence. Choice D is incorrect because *these fears* should appear closely after the first mention of fears; at the end of the second paragraph is too far removed. This leaves choice B as the clearest, most logical place for the addition.

SECTION THREE

MATHEMATICS

AN INTRODUCTION TO THE TSIA2 MATHEMATICS TEST

The TSIA2 Mathematics test contains 20 multiple-choice questions, covering a variety of topics from mathematics.

The four areas of focus are:

- **Quantitative Reasoning:** This category includes 6 questions that cover topics such as ratios, percentages, and rational numbers.
- **Algebraic Reasoning:** This category includes 7 questions that focus on topics in algebra, including linear equations, inequalities, and functions.
- **Geometric and Spatial Reasoning:** This category includes 3 questions that touch on geometric concepts such as area, perimeter, and triangle properties.
- **Probabilistic and Statistical Reasoning:** This category includes 4 questions and covers topics such as probability and data analysis.

NOTES:

_____

_____

_____

_____

_____

_____

_____

_____

USING THE CALCULATOR

Calculators are frequently allowed for use on math tests, and the TSIA2 is no exception. However, there are a few things to keep in mind:

- The TSIA2 Mathematics test will provide a digital calculator for you to use during the exam.
- The calculator will change in functionality throughout the test, ranging from a basic four-function calculator to a graphing calculator.
- The calculator is not provided for every question, so you can't rely on it.
- You cannot bring your own calculator to the test.

With those points in mind, we will focus on strategies that do not make much use of the calculator. Instead, we will make use of your scratch board and some effective techniques. If you are allowed to use the calculator on a question, consider it your chance to **double-check** your work.

NOTES:

_____

_____

_____

_____

_____

_____

_____

_____

_____

_____

How to Take the Mathematics Test

The Mathematics test is organized a little differently than the other two tests on the TSIA2, but you will still need an overall approach for your foundation.

The Mathematics Game Plan

1. **Identify the Question Type**

   There are three types of questions on the Mathematics test: **Computation**, **Word Problems**, and **Graphs and Figures.** You'll learn more specific strategies later in this chapter.

   It will also help to determine the **content area** for the questions, such as *Pythagorean Theorem* or *averages*.

2. **Set Up Your Scratch Work**

   No matter the type of problem, you'll need to **write down important information** on your scratch board.

   Some questions will even require that you completely translate them into a new format before doing any work.

3. **Use the Right Strategy**

   Determine the solution you need to answer the question. If you are stuck, try to use one of the strategies covered in this book to help you work your way through the problem.

   Remember, you have the necessary time to try different approaches until something works.

   If you get totally stuck, use the **process of elimination** to make an educated guess.

4. **Double-Check Your Work**

   Not all math questions will allow you to use a calculator, so it is easy to make a simple mistake that could cost you some points. Make sure to check the following before you select your official answer:

   - Did you set the math up right?
   - Did you follow all of the steps?
   - Reread the question and make sure you solved what the question asked you to solve.
   - Check your negatives as well as technical processes, such as distribution or long division.

NOTES:

_____

_____

_____

THREE QUESTION TYPES

Before you focus too much on learning the specific rules of math that show up on the TSIA2, you need to learn a basic strategy for each of the **three question formats** you will see on the test.

- **Computation:** These questions are pretty short and get straight to the math without any context.
- **Word Problems:** These questions are usually longer and require you to translate a scenario into math before you can solve the problem.
- **Graphs and Figures:** These questions appear in multiple content areas and provide you with a table or some other figure.

The first question type we are going to tackle is **Computation**. Attempt the three questions on the next page to see how they work.

NOTES:

_____

_____

_____

_____

_____

_____

_____

_____

_____

_____

SECTION THREE, MATHEMATICS:
COMPUTATION

COMPUTATION, PRACTICE SET ONE

Question 1 of 9
If $6x + 4 = 20 - 2x$, then $8x =$

Answers	
A	2
B	16
C	24
D	32

Question 2 of 9
If a is the greater of two consecutive even integers, which of the following represents the sum of the two integers?

Answers	
A	$a - 1$
B	$a - 2$
C	$2a - 1$
D	$2a - 2$

Question 3 of 9
Which of the following expressions is equivalent to $4x^2 + 8x - 60$?

Answers	
A	$(x - 10)(x + 6)$
B	$(x + 10)(x - 6)$
C	$4(x - 5)(x + 3)$
D	$4(x + 5)(x - 3)$

THE COMPUTATION BASIC STRATEGY

Computation questions provide you with a straightforward math question without any tables, graphs, or real-world background. These questions are simply interested in your ability to **compute** a math problem.

THE BASIC STRATEGY:

1. **Copy the Question to Your Board**
   This step may seem unnecessary but remember that **Computation** questions are specifically designed to have trap answers based on you making an error.

   If you don't copy everything down, you might mess up something while you are looking from the monitor to your scratch work.

2. **Show Your Work**
   Whatever method you use to solve the problem, this step is important for the same reason as step one: if you don't show your work, you might skip a step or make an incorrect calculation.

   Note: Even if you get to use a calculator on a particular question, write everything down on your scratch board to keep track of the work.

3. **Double-Check Your Answer**
   After you solve everything, double-check your work and reread the question just to make sure you've done the right thing. Sometimes you can get lost solving the first step and not realize that you haven't finished the question! Watch out for:

   - **Careless Mistakes:** Classic examples include forgetting a negative, using the wrong operation, and misreading a number.

   - **Halfway Answers:** These are answers that result from working one of the steps in the problem but not the final solution.

4. **Guess if Necessary**
   Hopefully the first three steps have helped you solve the question, but if not, make sure to use a guessing strategy to choose an answer.

Let's use this approach on the first question.

Question 1 of 9
If $6x + 4 = 20 - 2x$, then $8x =$

Answers	
A	2
B	16
C	24
D	32

First, rewrite the important parts of the question. Then, work the steps out. It should look something like this:

$6x + 4 = 20 - 2x$

Add $2x$ to both sides.

$8x + 4 = 20$

Subtract 4 from both sides.

$8x = 16$

Divide both sides by 2.

$x = 2$

At this point, you may have been tempted to pick choice A. This is an example of a **halfway answer.** It represents the answer to x, but the question wants to know the answer to $8x$. Eliminate this choice immediately and finish the problem.

$8x = 8(2)$
$8x = 16$

Note that you could have ended up with either choice C or D if you made a **careless mistake** and either subtracted $2x$ or added 4 to each side instead of taking the correct step. It is **very easy** to do this, so be sure to show and check your work!

Try the computation strategy again on the following question:

If a number is chosen at random from the set $\{1, 2, 3, 4, \ldots, 18\}$, what is the probability that the number chosen is a factor of 17?	

A	$\dfrac{1}{18}$
B	$\dfrac{1}{9}$
C	$\dfrac{2}{9}$
D	$\dfrac{17}{18}$

NOTES:

_____

_____

_____

_____

_____

_____

_____

_____

_____

_____

_____

Even though this question uses a lot more words, the words are simply describing a math problem, not setting up a context, so this is just a **Computation** question. If you followed the steps correctly, your scratch board would look like this:

$$\{ \textcircled{1} \ 2, \ 3, \ 4, \ 5, \ 6, \ 7, \ 8, \ 9, \ 10, \ 11, \ 12, \ 13, \ 14, \ 15, \ 16, \ \textcircled{17} \ 18 \ \}$$

You can pretty easily **visualize** the information given to you in the question, which allows you to notice that 2 of the 18 numbers are factors of 17 (meaning they can be divided into 17 evenly.) With that in mind, the probability will be $\frac{2}{18}$, which reduces to $\frac{1}{9}$.

Notice that choice A would be attractive if you didn't write out all the numbers in the list. This is another example of why **showing your work** is really helpful on the math test.

NOTES:

_____

_____

_____

_____

_____

_____

_____

_____

_____

_____

PLUG IT IN

Plug It In is one of the best backup methods for when you're stuck on a question that is using variables, such as x or n. All you have to do is come up with your own numbers and try them out.

PLUG IT IN STRATEGY

1. **Does It Work?**
   You can't plug in numbers if you don't have any variables, such as x, somewhere in the problem. Check the question and the answer choices for any variables.

2. **Pick Your Number**
   Here are some tips on choosing a number:

   - Avoid 0 and 1

   - Pick 100 for percentages

   - Try 2, 3, or 5 if you're unsure

   - Just try something and try again if it doesn't work out—you have unlimited time!

3. **Solve the Problem and Circle the Output**
   Replace the variable in the question with your number and solve. The answer you get is the *output*. Make sure you **clearly mark** it on your scratch board.

4. **Use the Process of Elimination**
   Plug your number into each answer choice and **eliminate** any choices that do not produce a value that matches the output from the question.

   Your number will sometimes work with two choices. In that case, you'll need to **plug in again** (picking a different number) for the remaining choices only.

NOTES:

_____

_____

_____

_____

_____

_____

Let's practice using Plug It In on the second question from the exercise:

Question 2 of 9
If a is the greater of two consecutive even integers, which of the following represents the sum of the two integers?

Answers	
A	$a - 1$
B	$a - 2$
C	$2a - 1$
D	$2a - 2$

This question is pretty unusual because it's more of a description than a math problem, and there are variables in the answer choices. But these characteristics give us the perfect opportunity to use the Plug It In strategy.

First, pick a number for a and write it on your scratch board. Since a is even, make sure to pick an even integer and a value that will be easy to work with.

$a = 4$

Next, plug a into the problem and answer the question. We'll start by finding the value of the other even integer. If a is 4 and it is the **greater** of two consecutive even integers, the other integer needs to be 2.

That means the **sum** of the two integers is $2 + 4 = 6$. That's the output, so circle 6 in your scratch work.

Finally, you can plug your value into the answer choices. Your goal is to find an expression that, when you plug in 4 for a, equals 6.

Choice A: $a - 1$
     $(4) - 1 = 3$
Choice B: $a - 2$
     $(4) - 2 = 2$
Choice C: $2a - 1$
     $2(4) - 1 = 7$
Choice D: $2a - 2$
     $2(4) - 2 = 6$

Only choice D was equal to 6 when using 4 for the value of a, so that's our correct answer.

Try the next question on your own:

$x^2 - 3x - 15 = 13$

Which of the following values of x satisfies the equation above?

A	–7
B	–4
C	4
D	13

NOTES:

_____

_____

_____

_____

_____

_____

_____

_____

_____

_____

_____

_____

_____

The variable is in the **question** this time, and not in the answer choices. The main difference here is that we are going to **use the numbers in the answers**, instead of making up our own number. Note that the output value, 13, is already given to us as well!

Plug the value of each answer choice into the equation: $x^2 - 3x - 15 = 13$

Choice A: $(-7)^2 - 3(-7) - 15$
$49 + 21 - 15 = 55$

Choice B: $(-4)^2 - 3(-4) - 15$
$16 + 12 - 15 = 13$

Choice C: $(4)^2 - 3(4) - 15$
$16 - 12 - 15 = -11$

Choice D: $(13)^2 - 3(13) - 15$
$169 - 39 - 15 = 115$

Only choice B gave us the same output as the original question, so it is the correct answer.

NOTES:

_____

_____

_____

_____

_____

_____

_____

_____

_____

_____

FACTORING AND FOIL

Quadratic equations is a topic commonly found on the TSIA2 Mathematics test, especially as you score higher. The most common things you will need to do are **factoring** and **FOILing**, also known as distributing. We'll start by looking at how to **FOIL**:

FOIL stands for **F**irst, **O**utside, **I**nside, and **L**ast. This is a handy acronym to help you to remember how to distribute. Take a look at the following example:

$$(x + 2)(x - 3)$$

First: $(\boldsymbol{x} + 2)(\boldsymbol{x} - 3) = x^2$

Outside: $(\boldsymbol{x} + 2)(x - \boldsymbol{3}) = -3x$

Inside: $(x + \boldsymbol{2})(\boldsymbol{x} - 3) = 2x$

Last: $(x + \boldsymbol{2})(x - \boldsymbol{3}) = -6$

Put it all together and you get: $x^2 - 3x + 2x - 6$ which reduces to $x^2 - x - 6$

Let's use FOIL on question three from the exercise:

Question 3 of 9
Which of the following expressions is equivalent to $4x^2 + 8x - 60$?

Answers	
A	$(x - 10)(x + 6)$
B	$(x + 10)(x - 6)$
C	$4(x - 5)(x + 3)$
D	$4(x + 5)(x - 3)$

Instead of trying to factor the expression in this question, look at the answers. You can just **FOIL the answers** to find the correct choice:

Choice A: $(x - 10)(x + 6) = x^2 + 6x - 10x - 60 = x^2 - 4x - 60$

Choice B: $(x + 10)(x - 6) = x^2 - 6x + 10x - 60 = x^2 + 4x - 60$

Choice C: $4(x - 5)(x + 3) = 4(x^2 + 3x - 5x - 15) = 4x^2 - 8x\ - 60$

Choice D: $4(x + 5)(x - 3) = 4(x^2 - 3x + 5x - 15) = 4x^2 + 8x\ - 60$

When you distribute each answer choice, only the result in choice D matches the expression in the question, so it is the correct answer.

This page is intentionally left blank.

For the following question, you'll need to **FOIL** in reverse by factoring the polynomial. Give it a try on your own:

$2x^2 - 13x - 24$

Which of the following is a factor of the polynomial above?

A	$2x + 3$
B	$2x - 3$
C	$x + 8$
D	$x + 2$

NOTES:

_____

_____

_____

_____

_____

_____

_____

_____

_____

_____

_____

_____

This time, we have a polynomial and need to **factor** it. Start by writing placeholders for the factors on your scratch board. We will fill them in as we go:

$$(\quad)(\quad)$$

In this case, the $2x^2$ from the polynomial was created by multiplying the **first** terms in the factors. We can safely assume this was $2x$ and x. Fill this out in your placeholders:

$$(2x\quad)(x\quad)$$

The third term in the polynomial is -24, which is created by multiplying the **last** terms in the factors. There are several ways to arrive at -24:

1 and -24	3 and -8
-1 and 24	-3 and 8
2 and -12	4 and -6
-2 and 12	-4 and 6

The easiest way to figure out which pair of values works correctly is to simply try them out. Remember, you have time on the TSIA2 Mathematics test to work problems out carefully.

Plug in each set of values and **FOIL** the factors until you find the pair that works. The correct answer will match the polynomial in the question:

Incorrect: $(2x + 1)(x - 24) = 2x^2 - 47x - 24$
Incorrect: $(2x - 1)(x + 24) = 2x^2 + 47x - 24$
Incorrect: $(2x + 2)(x - 12) = 2x^2 - 22x - 24$
Incorrect: $(2x - 2)(x + 12) = 2x^2 + 22x - 24$
Correct: $(2x + 3)(x - 8) = 2x^2 - 13x - 24$

We can now conclude that the two factors of the polynomial are $(2x + 3)$ and $(x - 8)$, making choice A the correct answer.

NOTES:

_____

_____

_____

_____

_____

COMPUTATION, PRACTICE SET TWO

Question 4 of 9
The ordered pair $(a, b) = (4, -5)$ is a solution to which of the following systems of equations?

	Answers
A	$b = 2a - 13$ $b = a - 1$
B	$b = 2a - 13$ $b = a + 1$
C	$13 = 2a + b$ $1 = a - b$
D	$13 = 2a - b$ $1 = -a - b$

Question 5 of 9
Which of the following is a factor of $x^4 - 18x^2 + 81$?

	Answers
A	$x - 6$
B	$x - 9$
C	$x^2 - 3$
D	$x^2 - 9$

Question 6 of 9
$5(x + 6) + 5x + 5$ Which of the following is equivalent to the expression above?

	Answers
A	$5(2x + 7)$
B	$10(x + 3)$
C	$6x + 18$
D	$10x + 13$

ANSWER AWARENESS

If you preview the answer choices before solving a question, you can give yourself a head start. This is especially useful for questions that use exponents or distribution because the answer can be expressed in more than one way. You can also find clues that will help you solve a difficult question. We call this **Answer Awareness**.

Let's use **Answer Awareness** on question six from the practice set.

Question 6 of 9
$5(x + 6) + 5x + 5$ Which of the following is equivalent to the expression above?

Answers	
A	$5(2x + 7)$
B	$10(x + 3)$
C	$6x + 18$
D	$10x + 13$

Most students solve this question by distributing and combining like terms. Let's do that now. First, distribute:

$$5(x + 6) + 5x + 5$$
$$5x + 30 + 5x + 5$$

Combine like terms:

$$10x + 35$$

None of the answers look like this, so it's easy to get stuck. And, because students expect a simplified answer, many students ignore choices A and B and pick choice D because it's the only one with a $10x$.

To avoid this kind of problem, look at the answer choices *before* trying to solve the question and ask yourself this question: *what kind of mistake does the test think I'll make?*

You might notice that two answer choices include parentheses. The TSIA2 is probably using a factor to hide the correct answer. Pause a moment before picking your answer and see if you can factor anything out. In this case, we can factor out a 5 from both terms:

$$10x + 35$$

$$5(2x + 7)$$

Choice A matches this, so it is the correct answer.

Try the Answer Awareness strategy again on the following question:

$$\left(\frac{a^{-3}b}{b^2}\right)^{-1} =$$

A	$\dfrac{a^3}{b}$
B	$\dfrac{b}{a^3}$
C	a^3b
D	a^3b^{-2}

NOTES:

_____

_____

_____

_____

_____

_____

_____

_____

_____

_____

Before you panic over all of those exponents, take a breath and use Answer Awareness on the choices to figure out a plan. The answer choices tell you a few things:

- The terms are simplified, so you will need to combine terms.
- Two choices have a fraction, so you need to choose: keep or eliminate the fraction?
- All four choices use a^3 and three of the four use b, so you'll need to deal with the negative exponent.

First, combine the terms. Remember that we can only combine exponents that have the same base, so we need to focus on the b variable. When you have an exponent divided by another exponent, you can subtract the powers to combine them.

$$\left(\frac{a^{-3}b}{b^2}\right)^{-1}$$

Combine the variables by subtracting their exponents.

$$\left(a^{-3}b^{1-2}\right)^{-1}$$

Simplify.

$$\left(a^{-3}b^{-1}\right)^{-1}$$

At this point, if you don't know what to do with the negative exponents, you can use the answers as a guideline. All of the choices have a^3, so you can make an educated guess that $(a^{-3})^{-1}$ equals a^3. Use that same reasoning to say $(b^{-1})^{-1} = b^1$, which is equal to b.

Put everything together to clear out the negative exponents:

$$\left(a^{-3}b^{-1}\right)^{-1}$$
$$(a^3b^1)$$
$$(a^3b)$$

Choice C is the correct answer.

NOTES:

_____

_____

_____

_____

COMPUTATION, PRACTICE SET THREE

Question 7 of 9		Answers
If $5m - 6 = 3$, what is the value of m?	**A**	$\dfrac{5}{9}$
	B	$\dfrac{5}{6}$
	C	$\dfrac{6}{5}$
	D	$\dfrac{9}{5}$

Question 8 of 9		Answers
If there are 1.6 kilometers in 1 mile, how many kilometers are there in m miles?	**A**	$\dfrac{m}{1.6}$
	B	$1.6m$
	C	$1.6 + m$
	D	$\dfrac{1.6}{m}$

Question 9 of 9		Answers
Which of the following is NOT equivalent to $(2x - 6)(x + 3)$?	**A**	$2(x^2 - 6x + 9)$
	B	$2(x^2 - 9)$
	C	$2x^2 - 18$
	D	$2x(x + 3) - 6(x + 3)$

SECTION THREE, MATHEMATICS:
WORD PROBLEMS

WORD PROBLEMS, PRACTICE SET ONE

Question 1 of 9
If a marble is randomly chosen from a bag that contains exactly 6 purple marbles, 4 blue marbles, and 10 green marbles, what is the probability that the marble will NOT be green?

	Answers
A	$\frac{1}{5}$
B	$\frac{3}{10}$
C	$\frac{1}{2}$
D	$\frac{3}{5}$

Question 2 of 9
Last year, a surf shop gave s lessons on wake-boarding. This year, the surf shop gave five more than three times the number of lessons given last year. If next year the surf shop plans on giving twice the number of lessons it gave this year, how many lessons does the surf shop plan to give next year?

	Answers
A	$2s$
B	$3s + 5$
C	$6s + 5$
D	$6s + 10$

Question 3 of 9
Lilly and Laura pooled their money to purchase their brother, Liam, a video game for his birthday. The video game cost a total of $45. If Laura was only able to contribute $\frac{2}{3}$ of what Lilly did, how much did Laura put toward the present?

	Answers
A	$18
B	$21
C	$27
D	$30

THE WORD PROBLEM BASIC STRATEGY

Word Problem questions do more than just ask you to solve a basic math question. They will provide a short story or some kind of background information that you have to **translate** into math before you can solve it.

These questions are considered tough by a lot of people, but if you use a good strategy, they can actually be even **easier** than Computation questions.

THE BASIC STRATEGY:

1. **Read the Entire Problem**
   Before you do any math, you need to read the question. You don't want to start solving the wrong question and end up selecting a trap answer.

2. **Write Down the Actual Question**
   After you read the problem, write down the part where the problem **asks** you something. For example, if a question tells you about someone investing money into a savings account, it might ask you for the *starting investment* or it might ask you for the *total amount saved*.

3. **Translate the Words into Math**
   Set up all the math you need before you start calculating. Once the word problem is turned into a computation problem, you are set.

4. **Solve the Problem**
   Take your time to work everything out. It is easier to make a mistake on a word problem, so take it slow.

5. **Double-Check the Question**
   Before you make your selection, double-check the **question** to make sure you answered it correctly. It is easy to lose sight of the question and select a trap answer.

NOTES:

_____

_____

_____

_____

_____

Let's give it a try with question one:

Question 1 of 9
If a marble is randomly chosen from a bag that contains exactly 6 purple marbles, 4 blue marbles, and 10 green marbles, what is the probability that the marble will NOT be green?

	Answers	
A	$\frac{1}{5}$	
B	$\frac{3}{10}$	
C	$\frac{1}{2}$	
D	$\frac{3}{5}$	

The first thing to do is read the problem and write down the **question**: what is the probability that the marble is NOT green?

In order to find the probability of an event, we need to use the following formula:

$$\frac{\text{Number of desired outcomes}}{\text{Number of all possible outcomes}}$$

First, find the number of total possible outcomes by writing down and labeling the information given to you in the question: 6 purple, 4 blue, and 10 green, for a total of 20.

Next, find the number of desired outcomes by reviewing the question. Since the question wants to know the probability of drawing a NOT green marble, add up the number of **purple** and **blue** marbles.

Divide by the **total**:

$$\frac{6+4}{20} = \frac{10}{20} = \frac{1}{2}$$

If you consider the calculations you just did, you can see that the actual **math** part isn't too bad. The key is to get the **words** translated into **math**.

NOTES:

Try the basic strategy again with the following question:

Of the 22 families in a neighborhood, 3 have 1 child, 8 have 2 children, 6 have 3 children, 4 have 4 children, and 1 has 5 children. What is the median number of children in the 22 families?	

A	2
B	2.5
C	3
D	3.5

NOTES:

The question is asking what is the median number of children in the 22 families.

This question has a lot of information to track, and since it is asking for the median, we should do more than just rewrite the given numbers. We should write down the number of children for each of the families in a list:

$$\{1, 1, 1, 2, 2, 2, 2, 2, 2, 2, 3, 3, 3, 3, 3, 3, 4, 4, 4, 4, 5\}$$

Now, since the question wants to know the **median**, we need to find the middle values. Since we wrote it down, they are pretty easy to find:

$$\{\cancel{1}, \cancel{1}, \cancel{1}, \cancel{2}, \cancel{2}, \cancel{2}, \cancel{2}, \cancel{2}, \cancel{2}, \cancel{2}, 3, \cancel{3}, \cancel{3}, \cancel{3}, \cancel{3}, \cancel{3}, \cancel{3}, \cancel{4}, \cancel{4}, \cancel{4}, \cancel{4}, \cancel{5}\}$$

The middle two numbers are 2 and 3. When finding the median, if you have two middle numbers, you must find their **average**, so the median is $(2 + 3) \div 2 = 2.5$.

NOTES:

_____

_____

_____

_____

_____

_____

_____

_____

_____

_____

_____

TRANSLATING WORD PROBLEMS

We've already looked at the **Plug It In** strategy, but sometimes you will find it easier to just translate the words into an equation. Let's try that strategy on the second question from the exercise:

Question 2 of 9
Last year, a surf shop gave s lessons on wake-boarding. This year, the surf shop gave five more than three times the number of lessons given last year. If next year the surf shop plans on giving twice the number of lessons it gave this year, how many lessons does the surf shop plan to give next year?

	Answers
A	$2s$
B	$3s + 5$
C	$6s + 5$
D	$6s + 10$

After reading the problem and writing down the question, you should start translating the words into math.

The first sentence tells you that s represents the numbers of **wakeboarding lessons last year**.

The second sentence tells you that *this year*, the shop gave *five more than three times the number of lessons given last year*. Let's translate that:

> *five more*: $5 +$
> *three times*: $3 \times$
> *the number of lessons given last year*: s

Putting it all together, you get:

> $5 + 3s$

Now, before you select your answer, make sure you read the **question**: the question wants to know the expression for *next* year, which will be *twice* the value for *this* year.

> $2(5 + 3s)$
> $10 + 6s$

Therefore, the correct answer is choice D.

NOTES:

_____

_____

This page is intentionally left blank.

Try translating a word problem into an equation again with the following question:

Gloria collected s seashells from a beach. She placed 7 seashells on her desk as soon as she got home, and she divided the remaining seashells equally into 9 containers. If each container held 11 seashells, how many seashells did Gloria collect from the beach?

A	92
B	99
C	106
D	108

NOTES:

_____

_____

_____

_____

_____

_____

_____

_____

_____

_____

_____

Break the word problem into sections to make translating easier.

> *Gloria collected s seashells from a beach. She placed 7 seashells on her desk as soon as she got home*

We know Gloria started with s seashells and then took 7 away to place on her desk:

$$s - 7$$

Translate the next part of the word problem.

> *She divided the remaining seashells equally into 9 containers.*

Gloria took the leftover seashells, $s - 7$, and divided them into 9 containers. We can represent this with a fraction:

$$\frac{s - 7}{9}$$

Finally, take a look a look at the last part of the problem.

> *Each container held 11 seashells.*

We know each container holds 11 seashells, which tells us our fraction is equal to 11.

$$\frac{s - 7}{9} = 11$$

Now that we've translated the equation, solve it like a typical computation question and isolate the variable. First, multiply both sides by 9.

$$s - 7 = 99$$

Then, add 7 to both sides.

$$s = 106$$

NOTES:

_____

_____

_____

_____

_____

WORKING BACKWARD

When you get stumped by a word problem, it is a good idea to try **working backward** from the answers. This is similar to the **Plug It In** strategy, only there are no equations or variables.

Use the following steps to help keep you on track:

THE WORKING BACKWARD STRATEGY

1. **Identify the Question**
   Each answer choice is a possible answer to the question, so consider what the problem is **asking**. This will help you know how to work backward.

2. **Determine the Test**
   Before you try out the answers, determine which number you will use to **test** if they are accurate.

   For example, if a question wants to know how many pies were sold at a bake sale if the sale brought in $100 in sales, you would compare the output of each answer choice to **$100** as the test.

3. **Start with Choice B or C**
   The values in the answer choices are always listed in ascending or descending order. That means choices B and C represent the **middle** values.

   If you **start in the middle**, you can sometimes figure out if the answer choice is too big or too small, which will make the process easier.

4. **Check the Results Against the Test**
   Remember that the correct answer choice needs to pass the test you determined earlier.

5. **Use the Process of Elimination**
   Look for choices that don't pass your test. If you can determine that the answer choice was **too big**, eliminate it and all the larger choices. If the answer choice was **too small**, eliminate it and the smaller ones.

   If you can't determine which way to go, just eliminate the choice and move on to the next choice until you find the correct one.

Question 3 of 9
Lilly and Laura pooled their money to purchase their brother, Liam, a video game for his birthday. The video game cost a total of $45. If Laura was only able to contribute $\frac{2}{3}$ of what Lilly did, how much did Laura put toward the present?

Answers	
A	$18
B	$21
C	$27
D	$30

First, identify the question: *how much did Laura put toward the present?* This means that each choice represents a possible value for Laura's contribution to the present.

Next, identify the test: let's use the fact that Laura only contributed $\frac{2}{3}$ of what Lily did as our test.

Now, pick a choice and solve the question. Let's start with choice B. Since the question asks what *Laura* paid, choice B, $21, represents *Laura's value*. The question says the total cost was $45, so if Laura paid $21, we can deduce that Lilly paid the rest, $24.

Finally, check that these values pass the test. The question tells us that Laura only contributed $\frac{2}{3}$ of what Lilly paid. However, $\frac{2}{3}$ of $24 is $16, which is **not** what choice B says for Laura.

In fact, since choice B, $21, is larger than our test result, $16, we now know the answer is too **big**. Since choice A is the only choice smaller than choice B, it is likely the correct answer. You should now try choice A to confirm that it is correct.

Choice A says that Laura paid $18 for the present. Since the total cost was $45, Lilly would have paid $27 in this scenario. Since the test was the fact that Laura paid $\frac{2}{3}$ of what Lilly paid, we can confirm this answer: $\frac{2}{3} \times 27 = 18$. Since our value passed the test, we know we have the correct answer.

NOTES:

_____

_____

_____

_____

_____

Give Working Backward a try on another example:

A closet in the shape of a right triangle has an area of 25 square feet. If one leg of the right triangle that forms the closet is 5 feet longer than the other leg, what is the length of the longer leg?

A	5
B	7
C	10
D	15

NOTES:

_____

_____

_____

_____

_____

_____

_____

_____

_____

_____

_____

_____

Instead of creating a series of equations and solving, we should just try out the answers. Be careful that you read the question: the answers represent the **longer leg**. We are looking for an answer that gives a right triangle with an area of 25 feet.

Start with choice B again. Since the longer leg is 5 feet longer than the shorter leg, if the longer leg is 7 feet, then the shorter leg is 2 feet. Now, find the area using those two values: $\frac{1}{2}bh = \frac{1}{2}(2)(7) = 7$. Since our test was 25 feet, we know this answer is too small.

Cross off choices A and B. Try choice C next. If it is also too small, choice D will be the correct answer by default.

Choice C has the longer leg at 10 feet, which would make the shorter leg 5 feet. The area would be $\frac{1}{2}(5)(10) = 25$ feet, which is exactly right, making choice C the correct answer.

NOTES:

_____

_____

_____

_____

_____

_____

_____

_____

_____

_____

WORD PROBLEMS, PRACTICE SET TWO

Question 4 of 9
A local bakery sent out coupons to a customers, hoping to get as many shoppers to use them as possible. If the number of shoppers who did not use the coupon was 50 less than the number of shoppers who did use it, what fraction of the shoppers who received a coupon used it?

Answers	
A	$\dfrac{a - 50}{a}$
B	$\dfrac{a + 50}{a}$
C	$\dfrac{a + 50}{2a}$
D	$\dfrac{a - 50}{2a + 50}$

Question 5 of 9
An electronics store determines that in order to sell n gaming systems, the price per gaming system should be $p(n) = 60 - n$ dollars. Getting n gaming systems from the supplier costs the store $C(n) = 400 + 20n$ dollars. If the store's revenue from selling n gaming systems is $R(n) = n \cdot p(n)$, for what value of n will the store's revenue and cost be equal?

Answers	
A	20
B	15
C	10
D	0

Question 6 of 9
A group of 12 students bought muffins and coffee for breakfast. Each student in the group had either one muffin or one coffee. The muffins cost $1.75 each and the coffees cost $3.50 each. If the total cost of 12 breakfasts was $33.25, how many coffees were ordered?

Answers	
A	4
B	5
C	6
D	7

SYSTEMS OF EQUATIONS

A lot of word problems are secretly hiding a **system of equations**, which is a set of equations that share the same variables. Two clues in the word problem will let you know you're working with a system of equations:

- Two items that show up at least twice
- Enough values to set up two equations, usually six

Let's see how this works on question six from the practice set.

Question 6 of 9
A group of 12 students bought muffins and coffees for breakfast. Each student in the group had either one muffin or one coffee. The muffins cost $1.75 each, and the coffees cost $3.50 each. If the total cost of 12 breakfasts was $33.25, how many coffees were ordered?

Answers	
A	4
B	5
C	6
D	7

We see two items appear more than once in this word problem: **muffin** and **coffee**.

> A group of 12 students bought **muffins** and **coffees** for breakfast. Each student in the group had either one **muffin** or one **coffee**. The **muffins** cost $1.75 each, and the **coffees** cost $3.50 each. If the total cost of 12 breakfasts was $33.25, how many **coffees** were ordered?

We also have plenty of values to make equations: **12** students, **one** coffee or **one** muffin per student, **$1.75** for the cost of a muffin, **$3.50** for the cost of a coffee, and **$33.25** for the total cost.

NOTES:

_____

_____

_____

Translate the word problem into equations. Take it one piece at a time:

Equation One

A group of 12 students bought muffins and coffees for breakfast. Each student in the group had either one muffin or one coffee.

$m + c = 12$

Equation Two

The muffins cost $1.75 each, and the coffees cost $3.50 each. If the total cost of 12 breakfasts was $33.25...

$1.75m + 3.50c = 33.25$

NOTES:

_____

_____

_____

_____

_____

_____

_____

_____

_____

_____

_____

By building these two equations, you've created a **system**. There are a few ways to solve a system, but the best way on the TSIA2 is to use a method called **elimination**. It works like this:

1. Stack the equations so that the variables are lined up.
2. Multiply one or both equations by a constant.
3. Subtract one equation from the other.
4. Solve.

First, stack them up on your scratch board:

$$m + c = 12$$
$$1.75m + 3.50c = 33.25$$

Second, multiply one of the equations by a constant. The trick is to multiply one equation so the value in front of one of the variables is the same for **both** equations.

$$1.75m + 1.75c = (1.75)(12)$$
$$1.75m + 3.50c = 33.25$$

Simplify the first equation.

$$1.75m + 1.75c = 21$$
$$1.75m + 3.50c = 33.25$$

Next, subtract one equation from the other so that the m cancels out. You can reorder the equations before you do this to avoid negative values:

$$
\begin{array}{r}
1.75m + 3.50c = 33.25 \\
- \ 1.75m + 1.75c = 21 \\
\hline
0m + 1.75c = 12.25
\end{array}
$$

Finally, solve for c:

$$1.75c = 12.25$$
$$c = 7$$

Solving a system of equations means following several steps, and even more so if you have to solve for *both* variables in the problem. But remember: you have unlimited time! Take your time, follow the process, and you'll get it right.

NOTES:

_____

_____

Try it out on the following system of equations word problem.

Jennifer bought 2 cheeseburgers and 4 orders of fries for $15.50. Rachael bought 3 cheeseburgers and 2 orders of fries for $15.25. How much would 1 cheeseburger and 2 orders of fries cost?	

A	$5.75
B	$7.75
C	$9.50
D	$30.75

NOTES:

_____

_____

_____

_____

_____

_____

_____

_____

_____

_____

_____

First, translate the equations:

Equation One

Jennifer bought 2 cheeseburgers and 4 orders of fries for $15.50.

$2c + 4f = 15.5$

Equation Two

Rachael bought 3 cheeseburgers and 2 orders of fries for $15.25.

$3c + 2f = 15.25$

Stack the equations:

$$2c + 4f = 15.5$$
$$3c + 2f = 15.25$$

Multiply one equation by a constant to ensure a variable will be eliminated:

$$2c + 4f = 15.5$$
$$2(3c + 2f = 15.25)$$

$$2c + 4f = 15.5$$
$$6c + 4f = 30.5$$

Subtract the equations (after reordering):

$$6c + 4f = 30.5$$
$$- \; 2c + 4f = 15.5$$
$$\overline{4c + 0f = 15}$$

Solve:

$$4c = 15$$
$$c = 3.75$$

This word problem wants us to solve for more than one variable, so we also need to find the value of the fries. We can plug the value for cheeseburgers into either equation and solve for fries:

$$2c + 4f = 15.5$$
$$2(3.75) + 4f = 15.5$$
$$7.5 + 4f = 15.5$$
$$4f = 8$$
$$f = 2$$

Finally, answer the question: how much would 1 cheeseburger and 2 orders of fries cost?

$$c + 2f$$
$$(3.75) + 2(2)$$
$$\$7.75$$

WORD PROBLEMS, PRACTICE SET THREE

Question 7 of 9		Answers	
Biking at an average rate of 4 miles per hour, how many <u>minutes</u> would it take Sara to bike 1 mile?	**A**	4	
	B	15	
	C	20	
	D	30	

Question 8 of 9		Answers
Marya has 3 bills worth 10 dollars each and 4 bills worth 20 dollars each. If she chooses two of these bills at random, what is the probability that the two bills together will be worth at least 30 dollars?	**A**	$\dfrac{1}{7}$
	B	$\dfrac{3}{7}$
	C	$\dfrac{6}{7}$
	D	$\dfrac{41}{42}$

Question 9 of 9		Answers
Under specific conditions, the population of a particular bacteria doubles every seven years. If the population starts with 100 members, which of the following expressions would give the population of the bacteria t years after the start, assuming that the population is living under the specific conditions?	**A**	2×100^{7t}
	B	$2 \times 100^{\frac{t}{7}}$
	C	100×2^{7t}
	D	$100 \times 2^{\frac{t}{7}}$

SECTION THREE, MATHEMATICS:
GRAPHS AND FIGURES

GRAPHS AND FIGURES, PRACTICE SET ONE

Question 1 of 9

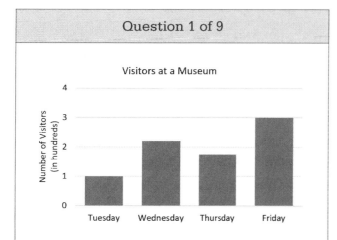

The bar graph above shows the number of people who visited a museum Tuesday through Friday of one week. If the number of visitors on Saturday was a one-fourth increase over the number of visitors on Friday, how many people visited the museum on Saturday?

Answers	
A	375
B	400
C	430
D	500

Question 2 of 9

The right triangle above has base x inches and hypotenuse y inches. In terms of x and y, what is the area, in square inches, of the triangle?

Answers	
A	$x\sqrt{y^2 - x^2}$
B	$\dfrac{x\sqrt{y^2 - x^2}}{2}$
C	$\dfrac{xy}{2}$
D	xy

Question 3 of 9

Which of the following points (x, y) lies on the graph of $12x + 3y = 30$?

Answers	
A	$(0, 1)$
B	$(2, 2)$
C	$(3, -7)$
D	$(4, -5)$

THE GRAPHS AND FIGURES BASIC STRATEGY

Some questions on the TSIA2 Mathematics test will provide information in a **graph or figure.** These questions can cover anything from basic geometric figures to reading a table.

All of the questions from the previous exercise included **Graphs and Figures** questions. Now let's look at the basic strategy.

THE BASIC STRATEGY

1. **Preview the Figure**
    Take a quick look at the graph or figure to see what information it contains. Don't try to memorize anything— just get your bearings.

    If the figure is a **shape**, you should **redraw** it on your scratch board and **label** it.

2. **Read the Entire Question**
    Most questions of this type have a lot of words and are, in fact, **word problems**. Take the same approach as before and read through everything before solving.

3. **Label or Write Down New Information**
    If the question provides additional details, such as the length of a side of a shape or numbers that will help you read a table, write it down on your board.

    You should also write down any **formulas** you will need at this point.

4. **Use the Figure**
    If the figure is too complex to copy down to your board, you will need to read the information from the screen. Make sure you are **extra careful** when you do this, and don't be afraid to use your finger!

5. **Estimate and Eliminate if Necessary**
    If you get stuck at any point in the question, take some time to make an educated estimate. Then mark your best guess and move on to the next question.

NOTES:

_____

_____

_____

_____

Let's take a look at the first question in the exercise to try out the basic strategy.

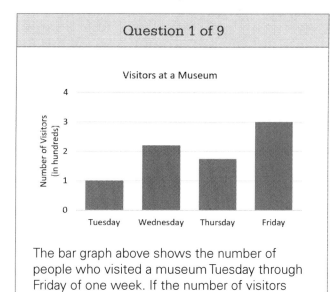

Question 1 of 9

The bar graph above shows the number of people who visited a museum Tuesday through Friday of one week. If the number of visitors on Saturday was a one-fourth increase over the number of visitors on Friday, how many people visited the museum on Saturday?

	Answers
A	375
B	400
C	430
D	500

First, look at the information displayed in the figure. The x-axis measures **days of the week**, and the y-axis measures the **number of visitors.** (Note that the y-axis is in hundreds, meaning 1 really represents 100. Keep that in mind.)

Now, look at the question. The **new information** is that *Saturday was a one-fourth increase over Friday*. The figure is too complex to bother rewriting, so just use your eye (or your finger) to find the value for Friday: 3, which really is 300.

Finally, increase this value by one fourth: $300 \times \frac{1}{4} = 75$. $300 + 75 = 375$, making choice A the correct answer.

NOTES:

Practice the basic strategy again with the following question:

Year	Lost	Won	Tied
2007	6	2	2
2008	8	0	2
2009	6	4	0
2010	4	6	2
2011	4	7	1
2012	5	5	2
2013	3	6	3
2014	2	10	0
2015	4	8	0
2016	3	8	1
2017	2	10	0
2018	1	11	0

A	2012
B	2013
C	2015
D	2017

The table above shows the regular season record of the Fort Worth Barracuda water polo team for their first 12 seasons. In which year did the Barracudas win their 30th regular season game?

NOTES:

_____

_____

_____

_____

_____

_____

_____

Start by **previewing** the figure. One thing you should notice before you read the question is that the years *increase* as you read *down* the figure, which is sometimes not the case. This could be important.

After reading the question, you should realize that you need to count the total wins, starting from the top of the table, until you get to 30.

2007: 2 total

2008: $2 + 0 = 2$ total

2009: $2 + 4 = 6$ total

2010: $6 + 6 = 12$ total

2011: $12 + 7 = 19$ total

2012: $19 + 5 = 24$ total

2013: $24 + 6 = 30$ total

This means that the 30th win happened during the 2013 season.

NOTES:

_____

_____

_____

_____

_____

_____

_____

_____

_____

_____

KNOW YOUR FORMULAS

If a question with **Graphs and Figures** asks you about a shape such as a rectangle, a circle, or a triangle, you will likely need to use a **formula.** Here is a list of common formulas you might need on your TSIA2 Mathematics test:

Area of a Square: $A = s^2$

Area of a Rectangle: $A = lw$

Area of a Triangle: $A = \frac{1}{2}bh$

Area of a Circle: $A = \pi r^2$

Circumference of a Circle: $C = 2\pi r$

Volume of a Cube: $V = s^3$

Volume of a Rectangular Prism: $V = lwh$

Volume of a Cylinder: $V = \pi r^2 h$

Pythagorean Theorem: $c^2 = a^2 + b^2$

Equation of a Line: $y = mx + b$

NOTES:

_____

_____

_____

_____

_____

_____

_____

_____

_____

_____

Look at question two from the exercise:

Question 2 of 9
y in *x* in The right triangle above has base *x* inches and hypotenuse *y* inches. In terms of *x* and *y*, what is the area, in square inches, of the triangle?

Answers	
A	$x\sqrt{y^2 - x^2}$
B	$\dfrac{x\sqrt{y^2 - x^2}}{2}$
C	$\dfrac{xy}{2}$
D	xy

First, **redraw** the figure and label it based on the question. There is no new information given in the question, but it does ask us to find the area of the triangle, which requires the **triangle area formula**:

$$A = \frac{1}{2}bh$$

To get started, plug in the value you know:

$$A = \frac{1}{2}(x)h$$

In order to the find the value of the other side (the height), you will need the **Pythagorean Theorem**:

$$a^2 + b^2 = c^2$$

For the Pythagorean Theorem, the a and b values represent the two legs, and the c value represents the **hypotenuse.** Plug in the information from the diagram and solve for the missing side:

$$x^2 + b^2 = y^2$$
$$b^2 = y^2 - x^2$$
$$b = \sqrt{y^2 - x^2}$$

Now, plug that value back into the area formula:

$$A = \frac{1}{2}(x)\left(\sqrt{y^2 - x^2}\right)$$
$$A = \frac{x\sqrt{y^2 - x^2}}{2}$$

Give it a try on the following question:

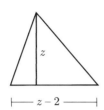

The area of the triangle above is 12. What is the value of z?

A	1
B	3
C	4
D	6

NOTES:

_____

_____

_____

_____

_____

_____

_____

_____

_____

_____

_____

_____

In this case, you can refer back to a method you've used before: **Plug It In**. Instead of writing down the formula and solving for z, try plugging the numbers into the problem to find what value for z gives you a triangle area of 12. Remember the area of a triangle formula is $A = \frac{1}{2}bh$:

Choice A: $A = \frac{1}{2}(1-2)(1) = \frac{1}{2}(-1)(1) = -\frac{1}{2}$

Choice B: $A = \frac{1}{2}(3-2)(3) = \frac{1}{2}(1)(3) = \frac{3}{2}$

Choice C: $A = \frac{1}{2}(4-2)(4) = \frac{1}{2}(2)(4) = 4$

Choice D: $A = \frac{1}{2}(6-2)(6) = \frac{1}{2}(4)(6) = 12$

Only choice D works, so it is the correct answer.

NOTES:

_____

_____

_____

_____

_____

_____

_____

_____

_____

_____

_____

EQUATIONS ON A GRAPH

Equations can be represented on a **graph** by drawing straight and curved lines. Sometimes, these questions don't give you a figure. In this case, your best bet is **not to draw one**. Look at the third question from the exercise as an example:

Question 3 of 9
Which of the following points (x, y) lies on the graph of $12x + 3y = 30$?

	Answers
A	$(0, 1)$
B	$(2, 2)$
C	$(3, -7)$
D	$(4, -5)$

Instead of trying to create your own graph, **plug in the answers**:

> **Choice A:** $12(0) + 3(1) = 3$
>
> **Choice B:** $12(2) + 3(2) = 30$
>
> **Choice C:** $12(3) + 3(-7) = 15$
>
> **Choice D:** $12(4) + 3(-5) = 33$

Only choice B produces 30, which matches the information in the question, so it is the correct answer.

NOTES:

_____

_____

_____

_____

_____

This page is intentionally left blank.

Try out this strategy on the next question. Notice that this time you have a figure you can use:

The graph of $y = f(x)$ is shown in the xy-plane below.

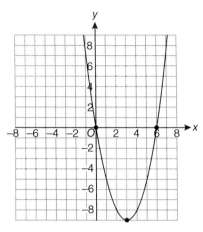

Which of the following equations could define $f(x)$?

A	$f(x) = x^2 - 6x$
B	$f(x) = x(x + 6)$
C	$f(x) = (x + 3)^2 - 9$
D	$f(x) = -x(x - 6)$

NOTES:

_____

_____

_____

_____

_____

_____

_____

_____

_____

We can take a similar tactic, only this time, we will use the numbers **in the figure** to test out the answers. Since we know that $y = f(x)$, we can pick a coordinate from the graph and plug it into the equation. Let's try $(6, 0)$, meaning when we plug 6 in for x, we should get 0 for the output y:

Choice A: $(6)^2 - 6(6) = 0$

Choice B: $(6)[(6) + 6] = 72$

Choice C: $[(6) + 3]^2 - 9 = 72$

Choice D: $-(6)[(6) - 6] = 0$

We ended up with two good choices, so now we need to try **one more point** for the remaining choices. Let's try $(3, -9)$ this time:

Choice A: $(3)^2 - 6(3) = -9$

Choice D: $-(3)[(3) - 6] = 9$

Only choice A works for both points, so it is the correct answer.

NOTES:

_____

_____

_____

_____

_____

_____

_____

_____

_____

GRAPHS AND FIGURES, PRACTICE SET TWO

Question 4 of 9		Answers

Which of the following is true about the line graphed in the xy-plane below?

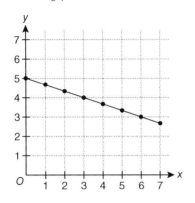

A	The line has a slope of $-\frac{1}{3}$ and contains the point $(3, 4)$.
B	The line has a slope of $-\frac{1}{3}$ and contains the point $(4, 3)$.
C	The line has a slope of -3 and contains the point $(3, 4)$.
D	The line has a slope of -3 and contains the point $(4, 3)$.

Question 5 of 9		Answers

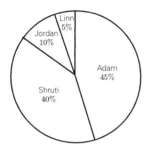

Adam, Shruti, Jordan, and Linn divided the cost of dinner as shown in the circle graph above. If Adam spent $6 more than Shruti on the dinner, how much did Jordan spend?

A	6
B	12
C	20
D	24

Question 6 of 9		Answers

A cubical box with edges of length g inches is enlarged so that the dimensions of the larger box are $g + 3$ inches, $g + 4$ inches, and g inches. The larger box has a volume that is how many cubic inches bigger than the volume of the original box?

A	$7g^2 + 12g$
B	$7g^2 + 12g + 12$
C	$14g^2 + 12g$
D	$14g^2 + 12g + 12$

DRAW IT OUT

Some questions on the TSIA2 will describe a figure using only words. This makes it difficult to use the Graphs and Figures strategy since you don't have anything to work with. Use the **Draw It Out** strategy as a bridge to get from the word problem to a place where you can apply the Graphs and Figures strategy.

Let's try it out with question six from the previous practice set.

Question 6 of 9
A cubical box with edges of length g inches is enlarged so that the dimensions of the larger box are $g + 3$ inches, $g + 4$ inches, and g inches. The larger box has a volume that is how many cubic inches bigger than the volume of the original box?

Answers	
A	$7g^2 + 12g$
B	$7g^2 + 12g + 12$
C	$14g^2 + 12g$
D	$14g^2 + 12g + 12$

This question describes a box that gets enlarged. Before you try to use the Graphs and Figures strategy, you should draw the smaller and larger versions of the box on your scratch board. (This is purposefully not drawn to scale. You don't have to be an artist to Draw It Out!)

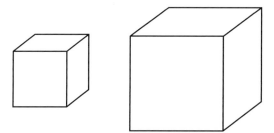

NOTES:

_____

_____

_____

_____

Next, review the question and label your figures. This question tells us the original box is a cube with sides of length g and the larger box has sides equal to $g + 3$, $g + 4$, and g.

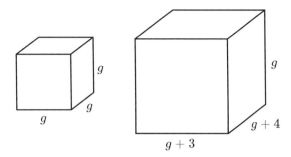

Since we are dealing with lots of variables, let's plug in 2 for g to make it easier.

Label the two boxes. Don't worry if your own drawing is not to scale:

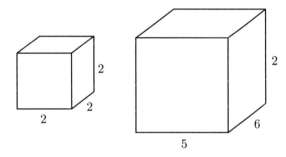

Now, we can solve the question just like a standard Graphs and Figures question. Find the volume of both shapes using the volume formula, $V = l \cdot w \cdot h$.

First, the original:

$$V_{\text{original}} = (2)(2)(2)$$
$$V_{\text{original}} = 8$$

Then, the enlarged:

$$V_{\text{enlarged}} = (5)(6)(2)$$
$$V_{\text{enlarged}} = 60$$

Next, answer the question. In this case, it asks us how many cubic inches bigger the larger box is than the smaller box. Use subtraction.

$$60 - 8 = 52$$

Finally, plug the value of g into each choice until one of them matches 52.

Choice A: $7g^2 + 12g$

Plug in.

$$7(2)^2 + 12(2)$$

Simplify.

$$28 + 24 = 52$$

Since 52 is the number we're looking for, we can stop here. If you want to be extra careful, you can test the other choices just to be sure, but choice A is the correct answer.

While drawing out a figure out won't solve the question for you, it will help you get to a point where you can use all the strategies you've learned for Graphs and Figures.

NOTES:

_____

_____

_____

_____

_____

_____

_____

_____

_____

_____

Take some time now to try the **Draw It Out** strategy on this next question.

If the dimensions of a rectangle are $x + 2y$ and $x - 2y$, what is the area of the rectangle in terms of a and b?	

A	$x^2 - 4y^2$
B	$x^2 - 8xy - 4y^2$
C	$x^2 - 8xy + 4y^2$
D	$2x^2 - 4y^2$

NOTES:

_____

_____

_____

_____

_____

_____

_____

_____

_____

_____

_____

Start by drawing the missing figure, a rectangle in this case:

Next, label it with the information given by the problem. Since there are several variables involved, let's plug in. Set x equal to 5 and y to 2 and find the sides of the rectangle:

$x + 2y$
$(5) + 2(2) = 9$

$x - 2y$
$(5) - 2(2) = 1$

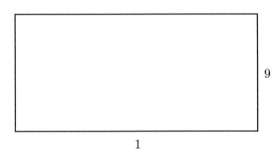

Find the area of the rectangle using the area formula, $A = l \cdot w$:

$$A = (1)(9) = 9$$

Finally, plug 5 in for x and 2 in for y in the answer choices until you find one that equals 9:

Choice A: $x^2 - 4y^2$

Plug in:

$$(5)^2 - 4(2)^2$$

Simplify:

$$25 - 16 = 9$$

Since choice A matches the value we found in the problem, we can stop there or check the other answers to be safe. In either case, choice A is the correct answer.

GRAPHS AND FIGURES, PRACTICE SET THREE

Question 7 of 9		Answers	
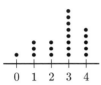 The dot plot above identifies the number of televisions in each of **20** households in a residential complex. What fraction of the households have fewer than two televisions?	**A**	$\dfrac{1}{10}$	
	B	$\dfrac{3}{20}$	
	C	$\dfrac{1}{5}$	
	D	$\dfrac{2}{5}$	

Question 8 of 9		Answers	
In the xy-plane, what is the y-intercept of the equation $y = 4(x + \dfrac{1}{2})(x - 5)$?	**A**	-10	
	B	-5	
	C	$\dfrac{1}{2}$	
	D	10	

Question 9 of 9		Answers	
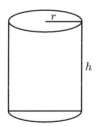 The formula for the volume of a right circular cylinder is $V = \pi r^2 h$. If $r = 3c$ and $h = 4c + 2$, what is the volume of the cylinder in terms of c?	**A**	$12\pi c^2 + 6\pi c$	
	B	$36\pi c^3 + 18\pi c^2$	
	C	$36\pi^2 c^3 + 18\pi^2 c^2$	
	D	$48\pi c^3 + 24\pi c^2 + 48\pi c$	

MATHEMATICS WRAP-UP

Remember the following key points when you take the Mathematics test on the TSIA2:

- Use the **basic strategy** for each question type:
  - **Computation**
  - **Word Problems**
  - **Graphs and Figures**
- Apply the different strategies covered in this chapter:
  - Plug It In
  - Answer Awareness
  - Translating Word Problems
  - Working Backward
  - Draw It Out

For further practice, check accuplacerpractice.collegeboard.org.

NOTES:

_____

_____

_____

_____

_____

_____

_____

_____

_____

MATHEMATICS ANSWER EXPLANATIONS

COMPUTATION, PRACTICE SET ONE

1. **The correct answer is B.** Start by isolating x. Then plug in the value for x into $8x$ and solve.

    $6x + 4 = 20 - 2x$
    $8x = 16$

    Since $8x$ is already isolated on one side, you can stop here with the correct answer. Alternatively, you could continue through with the full calculation to check your work.

    $x = 2$
    $8(2) = 16$

2. **The correct answer is D.** If a is the greater of two consecutive even integers, then the lesser of the two integers is $a - 2$. This is because consecutive even integers always have a difference of 2. Sum the two values to find the answer:

    $a + (a - 2)$
    $2a - 2$

3. **The correct answer is D.** Factor the expression.

    $4x^2 + 8x - 60$
    $4(x^2 + 2x - 15)$
    $4(x + 5)(x - 3)$

COMPUTATION, PRACTICE SET TWO

4. **The correct answer is D.** Plug in the values for the variables given into the answer choices. Start with the simpler second equation in each choice.

    $b = a - 1$
    $(-5) = (4) - 1$
    $-5 = 3$

    This cannot be true, so choice A can be eliminated.

    $b = a + 1$
    $(-5) = (4) + 1$
    $-5 = 5$

    This cannot be true, so choice B can be eliminated.

    $1 = a - b$
    $1 = (4) - (-5)$
    $1 = 4 + 5$
    $1 = 9$

This cannot be true, so choice C can be eliminated.

$$1 = -a - b$$
$$1 = -(4) - (-5)$$
$$1 = -4 + 5$$
$$1 = 1$$

This expression is true, making choice D the correct answer. Check your work by plugging in the values for the first equation into answer choice D.

$$13 = 2a - b$$
$$13 = 2(4) - (-5)$$
$$13 = 8 + 5$$
$$13 = 13$$

5. **The correct answer is D.** Factor the equation. Determine which two factors of 81 also add up to -18. The signs will need to be the same since the third term is positive.

$$x^4 - 18x^2 + 81$$
$$(x^2 - 9)(x^2 - 9)$$

This can be further factored to $(x + 3)(x - 3)(x + 3)(x - 3)$. However, only $x^2 - 9$ is listed as an answer option, so choice D is the correct answer.

6. **The correct answer is A.** Notice that 5 is a factor of each term in the expression $5(x + 6) + 5x + 5$. Begin by factoring 5 from each term and simplify.

$$5(x + 6) + 5x + 5$$
$$5[(x + 6) + x + 1]$$
$$5(x + 6 + x + 1)$$
$$5(2x + 7)$$

COMPUTATION, PRACTICE SET THREE

7. **The correct answer is D.** Add 6 to both sides of the equation to begin isolating m:

$$5m - 6 = 3$$
$$5m = 9$$

Divide both sides by 5:

$$m = \frac{9}{5}$$

8. **The correct answer is B.** To determine the equation, set up a proportion. For every 1.6 kilometers, there is 1 mile. This can be represented by a ratio:

$$\frac{1.6 \text{ kilometers}}{1 \text{ mile}}$$

The question wants to know how many *kilometers* there are in m miles, so set up a second ratio using variables:

$$\frac{k \text{ kilometers}}{m \text{ miles}}$$

To find the kilometers in terms of m, set the two ratios equal to each other and solve for k.

$$\frac{1.6 \text{ kilometers}}{1 \text{ mile}} = \frac{k \text{ kilometers}}{m \text{ miles}}$$

Cross-multiply.

$$(1.6)(m) = k(1)$$

Simplify.

$$1.6m = k$$

Therefore, there are $1.6m$ kilometers in m miles.

9. **The correct answer is A.** Simplify the expression through distribution.

Distribute:

$$(2x - 6)(x + 3)$$
$$2x^2 - 6x + 6x - 18$$

Collect like terms:

$$2x^2 - 18$$

Simplify each answer choice in a similar way and select the choice that does *not* equal the expression given by the question.

Choice A:	$2(x^2 - 6x + 9)$	
	$2x^2 - 12x + 18$	

Choice B:	$2(x^2 - 9)$	
	$2x^2 - 18$	

Choice C:	$2x^2 - 18$

Choice D:	$2x(x + 3) - 6(x + 3)$	
	$2x^2 + 6 - 6x - 18$	
	$2x^2 - 18$	

Only choice A does *not* match the original expression, so it is the correct answer.

WORD PROBLEMS, PRACTICE SET ONE

1. **The correct answer is C.** Probability is calculated as the number of desired outcomes divided by the number of total possible outcomes. In this problem, there are 10 desired outcomes. Drawing any of the 6 purple marbles or 4 blue marbles is desired: $6 + 4 = 10$. The number of total possible outcomes is the sum of the purple, blue, and green marbles: $6 + 4 + 10 = 20$ marbles in the bag. So, the probability of the marble NOT being green is $10 \div 20 = \frac{1}{2}$.

2. **The correct answer is D.** Write an equation for the number of lessons given this year. Then, multiply it by two to find the number of lessons expected for next year.

> Number of lessons last year: s
> Number of lessons this year: $5 + 3s$
> Number of lessons next year: $2(5 + 3s) = 10 + 6s = 6s + 10$

3. **The correct answer is A.** Translate the word problem into an equation and solve. Let y represent the amount Lilly contributed to the present.

$$45 = y + \frac{2}{3}y$$

$$45 = \frac{5}{3}y$$

$$27 = y$$

Lilly contributed $27, meaning that Laura contributed $\frac{2}{3}$ of this, or $18.

WORD PROBLEMS, PRACTICE SET TWO

4. **The correct answer is C.** Let x represent the number of shoppers who did not use the coupon and y represent the number of shoppers who did. Then $x = y - 50$ and $a = x + y$. Substitute the first equation into the second.

$$x = y - 50$$
$$a = x + y$$
$$a = (y - 50) + y$$
$$a = 2y - 50$$

Solve for y to determine the number of shoppers who did use the coupon.

$$a = 2y - 50$$

$$a + 50 = 2y$$

$$y = \frac{a + 50}{2}$$

The question asks for the fraction of shoppers who did use the coupon, or $y \div a$. Substitute in the expression for y.

$$\frac{a + 50}{2} \div a = \frac{a + 50}{2a}$$

5. **The correct answer is A.** To find n when revenue equals cost, set the equation for revenue equal to the equation for cost and solve for n. The equation for revenue includes $p(n)$, so plug the equation for price in for $p(n)$.

$$C(n) = R(n)$$
$$400 + 20n = n \cdot p(n)$$
$$400 + 20n = n(60 - n)$$
$$400 + 20n = 60n - n^2$$
$$n^2 - 60n + 400 + 20n = 0$$
$$n^2 - 40n + 400 = 0$$
$$(n - 20)(n - 20) = 0$$
$$n = 20$$

6. **The correct answer is D.** Set up a system of equations. Let m represent the number of muffins and c represent the number of coffees.

If there are 12 students who each bought a muffin or coffee, then $m + c = 12$. If the total cost was $33.25, then $1.75m + 3.50c = 33.25$.

Use substitution to solve for c, the number of coffees.

$m + c = 12$
$1.75m + 3.50c = 33.25$
$1.75(12 - c) + 3.50c = 33.25$
$21 - 1.75c + 3.50c = 33.25$
$1.75c = 12.25$
$c = 7$

WORD PROBLEMS, PRACTICE SET THREE

7. **The correct answer is B.** Determine how many hours it would take Sara to bike 1 mile traveling at 4 miles per hour. Distance = Rate × Time, so plug in the values for distance and rate provided and solve for time:

Plug the values into the formula. Sara's rate is 4 miles per hour, and the distance is 1 mile.

$D = rt$
$1 = 4t$

Divide both sides by 4.

$0.25 = t$

Convert 0.25 hours into minutes.

0.25×60 minutes $= 15$ minutes

It takes Sara 15 minutes to travel 1 mile going 4 miles per hour.

8. **The correct answer is C.** To find the probability of selecting two bills worth at *least* 30 dollars, first find the probability of selecting two bills worth *less than* 30 dollars. There are four possible ways to select the two bills, based on the order they are selected.

$10 then $10
$10 then $20
$20 then $10
$20 then $20

Of these possibilities, only one results in a selection worth *less* than 30 dollars: $10 then $10. To find the probability of selecting two $10 bills consecutively, first find the probability of selecting them individually.

There are three $10 bills and seven bills in total. Therefore, there is a $\frac{3}{7}$ chance of choosing a $10 bill as the *first* selection.

After selecting a $10 bill, there are two $10 bills remaining and six bills in total. Therefore, there is a $\frac{2}{6}$ chance of choosing a $10 bill as the *second* selection.

Multiply the two probabilities together to determine the chance of pulling the two $10 bills consecutively:

$$\frac{3}{7} \times \frac{2}{6} = \frac{3}{21}$$

Reduce the fraction:

$$\frac{1}{7}$$

Since $\frac{1}{7}$ represents the probability of selecting two bills worth *less* than $30, the probability of selecting two bills worth *at least* $30 is $\frac{6}{7}$.

9.   **The correct answer is D.** Translate the word problem into an expression. The starting population is 100, and it will double every seven years, so after seven years the population will be $100 \times 2 = 200$. Because this happens every *seven* years, a pattern can be established.

   7 years: 100×2

   14 years: 100×2^2

   21 years: 100×2^3

   28 years: 100×2^4

   ...

Account for the seven years it takes to double the population by raising 2 to the $\frac{t}{7}$ power, where t represents the number of years after the start of the population growth.

   t years: $100 \times 2^{\frac{t}{7}}$

GRAPHS AND FIGURES, PRACTICE SET ONE

1.   **The correct answer is A.** There were 300 visitors to the museum on Friday. Increase this value by one-fourth to find the number of visitors on Saturday.

   $$300 + 0.25(300) = 375$$

2.   **The correct answer is B.** The area of a triangle is found using the formula $A = \frac{bh}{2}$. The figure gives a value for the base of the triangle but not the height. Use the Pythagorean Theorem to find the height in terms of x and y.

   $$x^2 + h^2 = y^2$$

   $$h^2 = y^2 - x^2$$

   $$h = \sqrt{y^2 - x^2}$$

Find the area of the triangle by plugging in the expressions for base and height.

   $$A = \frac{bh}{2} = \frac{x\sqrt{y^2 - x^2}}{2}$$

3. **The correct answer is B.** Test each of the given points in the equation $12x + 3y = 30$.

    $$12(0) + 3(1) = 0 + 3 = 3$$
    $$12(2) + 3(2) = 24 + 6 = 30$$
    $$12(3) + 3(-7) = 36 - 21 = 15$$
    $$12(4) + 3(-5) = 48 - 15 = 33$$

    Only the point $(2, 2)$ solves the equation correctly, so it is on the graph of the equation.

GRAPHS AND FIGURES, PRACTICE SET TWO

4. **The correct answer is A.** Notice from the figure that the line passes through the points $(3, 4)$ and $(0, 5)$. Find the slope using these points:

    $$m = \frac{y_2 - y_1}{x_2 - x_1} = \frac{5 - 4}{0 - 3} = -\frac{1}{3}$$

    The line has a slope of $-\frac{1}{3}$ and passes through the point $(3, 4)$.

5. **The correct answer is B.** Let x represent the total cost of the dinner. Adam's share is $0.45x$, Shruti's share is $0.40x$, Jordan's share is $0.10x$, and Linn's share is $0.05x$. Write an expression to show that Adam spent $6 more than Shruti and solve for x.

    $$0.45x = 0.40x + 6$$
    $$0.05x = 6$$
    $$x = 120$$

    The total cost of the dinner was $120. To determine what Jordan spent, plug in 120 for x into the expression for Jordan's share.

    $$0.10(120) = \$12$$

6. **The correct answer is A.** Volume can be found using the formula $V = lwh$. Since the original box is a cube, the length, width, and height are all g. Therefore, its volume is $V_1 = g^3$. Use the new values to find the volume of the larger box.

    $$V = lwh$$
    $$V_2 = g(g + 3)(g + 4)$$
    $$V_2 = (g^2 + 3g)(g + 4)$$
    $$V_2 = g^3 + 4g^2 + 3g^2 + 12g$$
    $$V_2 = g^3 + 7g^2 + 12g$$

    Subtract V_1 from V_2 to find the increase in size.

    $$V_2 - V_1 = (g^3 + 7g^2 + 12g) - g^3 = 7g^2 + 12g$$

GRAPHS AND FIGURES, PRACTICE SET THREE

7. **The correct answer is C.** Determine which households have fewer than two televisions. According to the chart, the only households with fewer than two televisions are those with zero or one television. There is one household with zero televisions and three households with one television, so $1 + 3 = 4$ total households with fewer than two televisions.

    Because there are a total of 20 households, the fraction of them with fewer than two televisions is $\frac{4}{20}$, which reduces to $\frac{1}{5}$.

8. **The correct answer is A.** To determine the y-intercept, plug 0 in for x and solve:

    $$y = 4(x + \frac{1}{2})(x - 5)$$

    $$y = 4(0 + \frac{1}{2})(0 - 5)$$

    Simplify.

    $$y = 4(\frac{1}{2})(-5)$$

    $$y = -10$$

9. **The correct answer is B.** To find the volume of the cylinder, plug the value of the radius $(3c)$ and the value of the height $(4c + 2)$ into the formula for the volume of a cylinder provided by the question:

    $$V = \pi r^2 h$$
    $$V = \pi (3c)^2 (4c + 2)$$

    Simplify.

    $$V = \pi (9c^2)(4c + 2)$$

    Distribute.

    $$V = \pi (36c^3 + 18c^2)$$
    $$V = 36\pi c^3 + 18\pi c^2$$

SECTION FOUR

WRAP-UP

REMEMBER THESE KEY TEST-TAKING TECHNIQUES

- **Take Your Time:** The TSIA2 is untimed, so take your time to work every question and read every passage carefully.

- **Use Mental Breaks:** Use mental breaks to pace yourself through the exam so you don't feel overwhelmed.

- **Process of Elimination:** Eliminate incorrect answer choices whenever you can, especially if you're stuck on a question.

- **Always Check Twice:** Double-check your answers on *every* section before moving on.

- **One at a Time:** The TSIA2 is adaptive, so you can only work the question in front of you; focus on the question you are working, and don't worry about what came before and what might come next.

NOTES:

_____

_____

_____

_____

_____

_____

_____

_____

_____

_____

_____

BEFORE THE TEST DATE

- Get **enough sleep** for about a week before your test.

- **Eat well** in the days leading up to the test.

- **Bring a snack** and plan to eat it in between the test sections.

- Get **mentally prepared** by focusing on your overall **game plan** just before you enter the testing center.

- Take the **pre-assessment** a few days before you plan to take the test.

- **Schedule the test** with the center; if they don't require scheduling, plan to **get there in the morning** so you have plenty of time to finish the test.

NOTES:

_____

_____

_____

_____

_____

_____

_____

_____

_____

_____

_____

CITATIONS

Section Two, ELAR: Short Passage

McFarland, J. Horace. "The Growth of the Oak." The Outlook, Volume 72, No. 9, 1902.

Section Two, ELAR: Long Passage

Dounce, Harry Esty. "Some Nonsense About a Dog." Harcourt, Brace, 1921.

Contributors

Chief Academic Officer

Oliver Pope

Content Editors

Allison Eskind

Peter Franco

Lisa Primeaux-Redmond

Content Proofers

Craig Gehring

Lauren Brecht

Stephanie Constantino

Eric Manuel

Lauren Miklovic

Natalie Mucker

Interior and Cover Design

Elaine Broussard

Jeff Garrett

Nicole St. Pierre